DUb.

TRAVEL GUIDE

2024

Navigating the Dynamic Metropolis of the
Arabian Gulf, from Luxurious Skyscrapers
to Rich Cultural Treasures, with Insider
Tips and Must-See Destinations

Mario A. Clark

TABLE OF CONTENT

INTRODUCTION

Discovering Dubai: An Overview

The Allure of the Arabian Gulf

The Arabian Gulf, a hub of modernity and history, has a seductive attraction that draws tourists in with its many facets. This area, which is located in the Middle East, is rich in historical value. Its ancient coastlines witnessed the expansion and decline of empires as well as the burgeoning of trade routes that linked East and West, leaving a lasting impression on its culture.

The Gulf's natural splendour is really breathtaking. Crystal-clear waves that sparkle in the all-year sun meet pristine beaches with fine sands. But the harsh desert vistas that reach into the distance provide a dramatic, mesmerising contrast, drawing attention away from the beach as well. Here, visitors can indulge in dune-bashing, camel riding, or just plain stargazing under the expansive Arabian sky. The diversity of civilizations in the Arabian Gulf is what actually sets it unique. From the peaceful desert Bedouin customs to the urban metropolises of Dubai and Abu Dhabi, the area skillfully combines traditional practices with contemporary goals. This ethnic richness is evident in the food, music, and festivals, providing tourists with a diverse range of experiences.

The Gulf region is an economic powerhouse. It has evolved into a major global financial and commercial hub thanks to its oil and gas riches. Architectural wonders, such as the recognisable Burj Khalifa, which is a testimony to human creativity, grace the skyline.

In the Gulf, living in luxury is the norm. Travellers enjoy lavish hotels and resorts, shoppers indulge in opulent malls, and foodies enjoy Michelin-starred cuisine. The Arabian Gulf's warmth and kindness, however, continue to be unmatched despite its grandeur. Visitors are welcomed with open arms by the locals, offering a really unique experience.

A variety of memorable activities await you on your trip to the Arabian Gulf, from thrilling desert safaris and exhilarating water sports to strolling through bustling souks and indulging in local cuisine. The attraction of the Arabian Gulf is a complex mosaic with many facets, each offering a unique view into a place where tradition and modernity coexist in perfect harmony. Be ready to be mesmerised as you begin your voyage since the Arabian Gulf is a place unlike any other where innovation, nature, and history come together in a captivating dance of opposites.

A Snapshot of Dubai in 2024

The gem of the Arabian Gulf, Dubai, has evolved into a cutting-edge metropolis that melds tradition and innovation effortlessly. In 2024, this innovative metropolis will keep pushing the envelope and providing tourists with a once-in-a-lifetime experience.

Dubai's skyline, with its architectural wonders that soar ever higher into the heavens, is a testament to human inventiveness. The Burj Khalifa, the tallest building in the world, is still a well-known representation of the aspirations of the metropolis. And now that the Dubai Creek Tower is almost finished and on track to surpass even the Burj Khalifa in height, it will once again transform the skyline.

Dubai's growth has made sustainability a defining characteristic. The city is a forerunner in sustainable urban living thanks to its extensive solar energy projects, environmentally friendly urban planning, and growing network of electric and autonomous vehicles.

The old Al Fahidi District in Dubai, where conventional architecture and heritage monuments have been meticulously conserved, is a prime example of the city's cultural renaissance. The city's rich history and thriving artistic scene are highlighted at museums and galleries, providing a view into its varied cultural identity.

Dubai continues to surprise with transportation advancements like the Hyperloop, which promises incredibly quick and effective transit both within the city and beyond. Electric autonomous vehicles are now frequently seen, easing traffic and decreasing pollution while offering a glimpse into the future of urban travel.

Luxury is still fundamental to Dubai. The city's lifestyle continues to be defined by top-notch shopping opportunities, Michelin-starred restaurants, and sumptuous lodging at the newest resorts, guaranteeing that tourists are engulfed in rich indulgence.

Cultural celebrations like the Dubai Shopping Festival and Dubai Food Festival, where many culinary traditions come together, celebrate Dubai's multicultural population.

The tourist experience has been improved by artificial intelligence's seamless integration into daily life. The city can be easily navigated thanks to chatbots and AI helpers that offer real-time information, tailored recommendations, and even immersive augmented-reality tours.

The entertainment scene in Dubai is a spectacle unto itself. With year-round international performances and cultural events, Expo 2020 leaves a lasting impression. Theme parks like IMG Worlds of Adventure and Dubai Parks and Resorts provide exhilarating experiences for visitors of all ages, while the Dubai Opera captivates audiences with its world-class performances.

Dubai in 2024 will be a city of unending innovation, eco-friendly living, cultural diversity, and extravagant luxury. Prepare to be entranced by the clash between tradition and modernity as you explore this city of dreams, where every turn offers a fresh and thrilling experience.

What Sets This Travel Guide Apart

In a world overrun with travel guides, "Dubai Travel Guide 2024" distinguishes itself as a necessary travel companion for those planning a trip to Dubai, the gem of the Arabian Gulf. This travel book stands out thanks to a thoughtfully chosen combination of knowledge, current data, and a strong respect for Dubai's distinctive character.

Local Insights: This book is filled with firsthand experiences and local insights, unlike conventional travel books. It was created by people who not only thoroughly studied Dubai but also have a deep appreciation for its intricacies and culture.

Current Information: Because travel is constantly changing, this book makes sure you have the most up-to-date knowledge for 2024. You can be sure that you're getting the most up-to-date information on anything from visa updates to recently opened restaurants and attractions.

No detail is overlooked in the comprehensive coverage provided by "Dubai Travel Guide 2024". It provides a thorough overview of all Dubai has to offer, whether you're looking for luxurious or affordable options, cultural activities or heart-pounding excursions.

Access insider knowledge and local knowledge to help you make the most of your visit. These tips will improve your experience in Dubai, from navigating the busy souks to comprehending cultural etiquette.

example Itineraries: Create your own journey with the aid of thoughtfully created example itineraries rather than merely following the crowd. These itineraries accommodate a range of interests and schedules, whether you have a week or only a few days.

Cultural Background: This guide offers more than simply a list of sites; it also explains their cultural backgrounds. Learn about Dubai's culture, history, and modern advancements to have a deeper understanding of the city.

Practical Resources: With information on visas, travel, lodging, and more, this book makes planning your trip easier and guarantees a pleasant experience.

Beautiful Design: In addition to its amount of information, the guide has a beautiful design with graphics, images, and maps that not only provide knowledge but also pique your wanderlust.

Passion for Travel: This travel guide's passion for travel and sincere desire to assist you in making lifelong memories are what distinguish it most. It's more than just a book; it's your dependable travel buddy.

CHAPTER 1

Planning Your Trip

When to Visit Dubai

The weather in Dubai has two distinct seasons: hot and even hotter, with the rare sprinkle of rain. Depending on your tolerance for heat and the type of experience you're looking for, there are different times of year to visit this busy city.

1. Winter Wonderland (November to February): Without question, the ideal time to visit Dubai is during the winter. The city now experiences nice mild days and chilly evenings as the sweltering summer heat retreats. Dubai comes alive throughout this time with outdoor activities, festivals, and outdoor dining. It's the ideal time to enjoy numerous outdoor activities without feeling like you're scorching, such as exploring the desert, shopping at outdoor markets, and dining al fresco.

2. Shoulder Seasons (March to April, September to October): The cool spring and early fall provide a respite from the sweltering summer and the busy winter. While there is a gradual increase in visitors

and temperatures start to rise in March, it is still tolerable for those who want to avoid the busiest times. There are many outdoor activities to enjoy and temperate temperatures in April and October, which makes them particularly pleasant months.

3. Summer Sizzle (May to August): The summers in Dubai are known for their intense heat, with daily highs far above 100°F (40°C). Due to the intense heat, this is the off-peak season, but it's also when you may get some fantastic prices on lodging. This could be a good time to travel if you're willing to put up with the heat or intend to spend the most of your time indoors.

The ideal time to travel to Dubai ultimately depends on your tastes and what you hope to see and do. The winter is the greatest time to visit Dubai if you want to enjoy a comfortable and lively experience. Consider travelling during the shoulder seasons if you want to save money and don't mind the heat. If you decide to venture out into the summer heat, just keep in mind to pack appropriately and stay hydrated.

Visa and Entry Requirements

Understanding the visa and entry procedures, which might change based on your nationality, the reason for your visit, and the length of your stay, is crucial before beginning your travel to Dubai. Although admission procedures to Dubai and the larger United Arab Emirates (UAE) are rather simple, compliance is essential to guarantee a hassle-free trip. Here is a summary of the major ideas:

1. Visa Categories:

Travellers who want to visit Dubai for pleasure, sightseeing, or family visits should apply for a tourist visa. Usually, it is good for 30 or 90 days.

Visa for Visit: Holders of this visa may go to Dubai to see immediate family members or relatives. Typically, it is good for 30 or 90 days.

Transit Visa: You can apply for a transit visa, which is normally valid for 48 hours if you have a layover in Dubai and intend to stay there for a brief period of time.

Residence Visa: Your employer or sponsor will often arrange for this visa if you intend to work or reside in Dubai.

2. Arrival-only visas

Visa on arrival is an option available to citizens of a number of nations. It is imperative to confirm the most recent information with the UAE embassy or official government websites before your journey as the particular list of permitted nations is subject to change.

3. Extensions of Tourist Visas:

If you already have a tourist visa and want to stay longer in Dubai, you can frequently do so without leaving the country.

Extensions are frequently given for an extra 30 or 90 days, but there can be charges.

4. Required Paperwork:

The following paperwork is normally required when applying for a visa to Dubai:

a finished visa application.

a passport that is valid for at least six months.

photos the size of a passport.

evidence of lodging in Dubai.

evidence that you have enough money to pay your stay.

Flight information and the travel schedule.

if there is a visa charge.

5. Promotion:

In many circumstances, especially for visit or tourist visas, you may need a local sponsor or host in Dubai. This sponsor may be a lodging establishment, a relative, or an acquaintance who resides in the UAE. They may also be asked to sign a sponsorship undertaking and frequently need to present an invitation letter.

6. Entrance stamps:

Immigration officers will stamp your passport with the proper visa or entry status when you arrive in Dubai. Make sure the visa you receive has the appropriate duration for your intended travels.

7. Overstaying Sanctions:

Dubai is serious about its visa policies. You could be subject to penalties, deportation, or entry prohibitions if you overstay your visa. It's critical to depart the country before your visa expires or, if required, to renew it.

Before your travel, make sure you are aware of the most recent regulations and visa requirements because they are subject to change. For the most recent information on visa and entrance requirements for Dubai, you can get in touch with the UAE embassy or consulate in your home country or visit the official UAE government website.

Budgeting and Currency

Setting a budget for your vacation to Dubai is an essential step in making sure you have a pleasurable and stress-free stay in this vibrant city. Although Dubai is famed for its grandeur, you can visit on a variety of budgets if you plan carefully. Here is a list of crucial budgeting advice and details on the money in Dubai:

1. Currency:

The UAE Dirham, sometimes known as AED, is the official currency of Dubai and the United Arab Emirates (UAE). It is frequently represented with the letters ". " or "AED."

2. Exchange rates:

Before exchanging money, it is a good idea to verify the current exchange rates because they can change. You can accomplish this at banks, exchanges, or by using apps that convert currencies.

3. ATMs and banking:

It is simple to get cash in Dubai because of its well-established banking infrastructure and abundance of ATMs. Despite the widespread acceptance of international credit and debit cards, it's a good idea to have some local currency on hand for smaller transactions or in case you visit locations that don't accept cards.

4. Affordable Accommodations

Although Dubai is known for its opulent hotels, there are other less expensive lodging options, such as hostels and guesthouses. To ensure the best rates, do your research and make reservations well in advance.

5. Eating

In Dubai, prices for meals might differ greatly. Local restaurants, food carts, and cafeterias offer reasonably priced meals.

Check out the various and delectable options in nearby markets and small restaurants for a fun experience that won't break the bank.

6. Transport:

Buses and the metro are both affordable and effective modes of transportation in Dubai. Consider getting a Nol Card, a contactless payment card with reduced bus and train prices.

7. Activities and Attractions:

To control expenditures, make intelligent plans for your operations. It's a good idea to verify pricing in advance and take into account package tickets if they're offered because some attractions charge admission. You can also visit free attractions like parks and public beaches.

8. Purchasing:

Dubai is a shopping mecca, but it's simple to go overboard. Establish a spending limit and adhere to it. Take advantage of sales events and think about haggling at traditional markets (souks).

9. Nightlife and entertainment

Although Dubai has a thriving nightlife, it can be pricey for drinks and entertainment at pubs and clubs. Look for happy hour specials and think about attending free events or cultural ones as entertainment.

10. Tipping: In Dubai, tipping is traditional. In restaurants, the service charge is frequently already included in the bill, but additional tips, typically between 10% and 15% of the total, are always appreciated.

11. Emergency Funds: It's a good idea to keep a reserve fund to cover unforeseen costs or crises. To cover unexpected events

like medical emergencies, think about purchasing travel insurance.

Packing Essentials

An exciting aspect of the adventure is getting ready for your trip to the Arabian Gulf. It's crucial to pack carefully and take into account the special features of this area to guarantee a smooth and comfortable journey. To ensure you have everything you need to make the most of your trip, here is a detailed list of what to pack:

1. Pack breathable, lightweight clothing, such as loose-fitting blouses, shorts, and dresses given the warm climate. A swimsuit is a must-have for resort pools and beach days.

2. Modest apparel: Although the Gulf is modern, it is respectful to wear modest apparel when visiting places of worship. If necessary, women should bring a scarf to conceal their shoulders and hair.

3. Sun protection: To protect oneself from the potent Arabian sun, you must wear sunscreen, sunglasses, and a wide-brimmed hat.

4. Comfy Footwear: For city exploration and participating in desert excursions,

comfortable walking shoes or sandals are a need.

5. Power Adapters: The Gulf region normally employs the British-style Type G plug, so be sure to pack power adapters and converters for your electrical gadgets.

6. prescriptions: Include a basic first-aid kit that contains necessities like pain relievers, antacids, and bandages, as well as any necessary prescription prescriptions in their original containers.

7. Toiletries: Even though the majority of hotels offer toiletries, you might want to bring your own brand. Include other necessities like a toothbrush, toothpaste, and toiletries.

8. Travel Documents: Make sure you have a printed itinerary, your passport, your visa, and any necessary paperwork for travel

insurance. Make digital copies of these and keep them in a secure location.

9. Travel Wallet: Keeping your passport, cash, and important papers organised and safe will be made easier with a travel wallet or pouch.

10. Cash: It's a good idea to have a combination of cash and credit/debit cards on you. Although there are many ATMs, certain local markets would prefer cash.

11. Language Resource: To make conversation easier, think about investing in a little Arabic phrasebook or language software.

12. Travel Locks: Travel locks for bags and daypacks will keep your valuables safe.

13. Universal adaptor: Even if British-style plugs are widely used, it's a smart idea to

have a universal adaptor on hand to charge various gadgets.

14. Reusable Water Bottle: Carry a reusable water bottle to stay hydrated. In most Gulf cities, tap water is generally safe, or you can purchase bottled water.

15. Entertainment: Pack novels, e-readers, or other pastimes for leisurely nights or downtime while travelling.

16. Camera and Chargers: Use a camera or smartphone to document your adventures. Don't forget to include plenty of storage, extra batteries, and chargers.

17. Travel pillows and eye masks can improve the comfort of long flights or road excursions.

18. Travel Insurance: Take into account comprehensive travel insurance that

addresses unexpected situations like medical emergencies and trip cancellations.

19. Small backpack or daypack: These are useful for transporting necessities for day trips and adventures.

20. Power Bank: With a portable power bank, you can keep your devices charged while you're on the go.

Health and Safety Tips

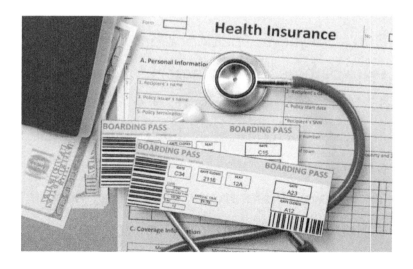

To have a stress-free and joyful trip to the Arabian Gulf, it is essential to ensure your health and safety. While visiting this dynamic area, keep in mind the following important health and safety advice:

1. Check Travel Advisories: For the most recent information and suggestions for the Arabian Gulf region, visit the government travel advisory website of your nation prior to your trip. Keep yourself updated on any dangers or issues that might arise.

2. Travel Insurance: Invest in full coverage of travel insurance that includes coverage for travel-related emergencies, trip cancellations, and medical emergencies. Keep a copy of your insurance information and emergency contacts with you at all times.

3. Vaccines and Health Precautions: Discuss any required vaccines or health precautions for your destination with your healthcare professional well in advance. Hepatitis A, B, and typhoid vaccines are examples of common vaccinations.

4. Prescriptions & Medication: If you take medication, be sure you have enough for the duration of your trip. Keep a copy of your medicines on you at all times, and if you have any special medical requirements, think about wearing a medical alert bracelet.

5. Hydration: The Arabian Gulf may be extremely hot, particularly in the summer. Drink plenty of water throughout the day to stay hydrated, and limit your intake of alcohol and caffeine to avoid becoming dehydrated.

6. Sun Protection: Use sunscreen with a high SPF, UV-protective sunglasses, and a wide-brimmed hat to shield yourself from the harsh sun. When the sun is at its fiercest, between 10 AM and 4 PM, exercise extra caution.

7. Respect Local Customs: Get to know the traditions and customs of the area, particularly with regard to attire and manners. When visiting places of worship, dress modestly and show respect for cultural customs.

8. Food and Water Safety: Even though the majority of businesses uphold strict food safety guidelines, it's best to eat at renowned venues. Use bottled water to consume and brush your teeth instead of tap water.

9. Exercise caution while choosing vendors for street food, even though it can be delectable. Choose hot, freshly cooked dishes over raw or undercooked ones.

10. Travelling Alone: If you're travelling alone, stay in well-lit, busy locations, especially at night. Tell someone you can trust where you are going and what you plan to do.

11. Petty Theft Prevention: Always keep your possessions secure, especially in markets and crowded areas. Cash and vital papers should be kept in a money belt or neck pouch.

12. Emergency Contacts: Save local emergency numbers for the police, ambulance, embassy or consulate of your nation in your phone and write them down on paper as well.

13. Transit Security: Use caution when taking cabs and public transit. Prior to leaving, select reliable providers and verify the cost of your trip.

Language Barriers: To help with communication in an emergency or while requesting assistance, learn a few basic Arabic words or carry a translation app.

15. Be Informed: Keep current with neighbourhood news and events while visiting, especially if you intend to visit isolated locations.

CHAPTER 2

Getting Around Dubai

Air Travel: Navigating Dubai International Airport

In addition to being one of the busiest airports in the world, Dubai International Airport (DXB) is a wonder of contemporary aviation infrastructure. Given its enormous size and the wide range of services it provides, navigating this busy hub may be an adventure in and of itself. Here is a detailed guide to assist you efficiently traversing Dubai International Airport and enjoying your flight as much as possible.

The DXB airport has three passenger terminals: Terminal 1, Terminal 2, and Terminal 3. The biggest terminal, Terminal 3, is used mostly by Emirates Airlines. While Terminal 1 serves many international airlines, Terminal 2 serves low-cost carriers and regional flights. Make sure you are aware of your departure location in advance.

2. Check-In: Online check-in is available from many airlines, which can help you save time at the airport. However, if you must

check in at the airport, get there early because queues can be lengthy, especially during periods of high travel demand.

3. Immigration and Security: Go through the immigration and security procedures after you've checked in. Make sure you are prepared with your passport, boarding pass, and visa paperwork. Although lineups can vary, the process is often efficient, so give yourself extra time.

4. Duty-Free Shopping: The Dubai Airport is well known for its vast duty-free selection. Luxury items, electronics, and regional goods can all be found in abundance in Terminal 3. Allow time to investigate, and keep your boarding card close by in case you want to make purchases.

5. Lounges: If you have access to airport lounges, DXB provides a variety of choices,

including independent lounges like the Marhaba Lounge and airline-specific lounges. Lounges are excellent places to unwind, enjoy some drinks, and work quietly.

6. Dining: The Dubai Airport offers a wide array of dining alternatives, from luxury restaurants serving a range of cuisines to worldwide fast food brands. Try some Middle Eastern specialities or indulge in old favourites.

7. Connecting Flights: If you have a connecting flight, look for your gate information on the departure screens. Due to the vastness of the airport, getting to your connecting terminal can involve taking an airport rail or bus.

8. Wi-Fi and charging: The airport offers free Wi-Fi so you can stay connected. Your

devices may be charged in many seating places, ensuring that you never run out of juice.

9. Access to the City: Dubai Airport has excellent transport options. Taxis, ride-sharing services, the Dubai Metro, and airport shuttles are all options. Find the mode of transportation that best meets your needs by doing some research.

10. Traveller Services: DXB provides a range of services to travellers, including currency exchange, medical services, prayer rooms, luggage storage, and even a Zen Garden for tranquilly.

11. Art & Culture: Get a taste of Dubai's artistic culture by exploring the airport's bright art installations and cultural exhibitions.

12. Terminal Services: Be sure to check out the lounges, shops and restaurants that are offered in your particular terminal as each one has its own amenities.

Public Transportation

The cities in the Arabian Gulf have created a sophisticated and effective public transit system that makes travelling around the cities easy. Public transit is a convenient and affordable method to get around, whether you're exploring the busy streets of Dubai, the picturesque neighbourhoods of Abu Dhabi, or other major centres in the area. Here is a list of the popular public transit options in the Arabian Gulf:

1. Metro: The metro systems in many Gulf cities are up-to-date and comprehensive.

For instance, Dubai features one of the most cutting-edge and practical metro systems in the world, the Dubai Metro. Key locations, such as popular tourist destinations, shopping centres, and corporate hubs, are connected by the metro.

2. Public buses are a dependable means of getting across cities and between them. They provide routes that the metro may not cover, providing them with a flexible transportation choice. The air-conditioned buses offer relief from the heat and have generally regular timetables.

3. Trams: Some cities, like Dubai, have tram networks to go along with their bus and metro systems. Accessing seaside areas and popular tourist destinations is made especially easy by trams.

4. Water Taxis and Ferries: Due to the waterfront sites around the Gulf, water taxis and ferries are frequently used as a form of transportation, particularly in urban centres like Dubai and Abu Dhabi. They connect several waterfront areas and offer beautiful vistas.

5. Monorails: In some locations, such as Dubai's Palm Jumeirah Monorail, which connects the Palm to the mainland, monorails are employed for efficient transit.

6. Taxis and Ride-sharing: Taxis are accessible and provide a comfortable means of transportation. The use of ride-sharing services like Uber and regional alternatives is common and can be practical for door-to-door commuting.

7. Nol Card (Dubai) or an equivalent: Smart cards are commonly used in the Arabian

Gulf region to pay for public transport. The Nol Card can be used seamlessly in Dubai on numerous types of transportation after being loaded with credit.

8. Accessibility: The Gulf region's public transit systems are built with accessibility in mind and include amenities like ramps, lifts, and spaces specifically dedicated to passengers with disabilities.

9. Operating Hours: Most public transit systems are open from early in the morning till after dark. However, plans may change during Ramadan and on some federal holidays.

10. Cost: There are alternatives for single excursions or daily/weekly passes that offer unrestricted travel within a predetermined window. Fares are often reasonable.

.

Renting a Car

For example, if you want the freedom to visit locations outside of city centres or want to visit sites outside of the Arabian Gulf region's urban centres, renting a car can be a practical and adaptable method to explore the region. What you should know before hiring a car in the Arabian Gulf is as follows:

1. Eligibility: Depending on the nation and rental business, you must normally be at

least 21 or 25 years old to rent a car in the Arabian Gulf. Additionally, you need to have a current driver's licence from your native nation. It's a good idea to verify the particular regulations of the country you plan to travel in order to determine whether an International Driving Permit (IDP) is necessary in some circumstances.

2. Rental Companies: The Gulf region is home to a large number of both national and local automobile rental businesses. There are both national rental companies and regional ones in the area, including well-known brands like Hertz, Avis, and Budget. Find the rental company that offers the greatest prices and services for your needs by doing some research and comparing them.

3. Making a Reservation in Advance: It's a good idea to make a reservation for your rental car, especially during the busiest travel times. Reservations can be made online or with travel companies.

4. Identification: You normally need to present your passport, driver's licence, and a credit card for payment and the security deposit while renting a car. Make sure you have enough credit on your credit card to cover the deposit, which is refunded if you return the automobile in working order.

5. Rental Insurance: Many rental businesses provide insurance packages that include liability, accident damage, and theft protection. Examine the available coverage options, then choose if you want to buy more insurance or rely on your current travel insurance to provide coverage.

6. Car kinds: Car rental companies provide a range of car kinds, from compact cars to SUVs and premium cars. Consider elements like the number of passengers, luggage capacity, and the type of terrain you'll be driving on when selecting a vehicle that will meet your demands.

7. Driving Regulations: Get to know the country you're visiting's driving laws and guidelines. For instance, within the Arabian Gulf region, different countries may have different speed restrictions, seat belt regulations, and drinking limitations.

8. Road Conditions: Gulf countries' roads are typically well-maintained and equipped with contemporary infrastructure. A GPS or dependable navigation programme on your phone might be really helpful because traffic signs and instructions might be in Arabic.

9. Fuel: Self-service at the pump is typical in the Gulf, where petrol is abundantly available. There are many petrol stations along important roads.

10. Parking: Major cities in the Arabian Gulf have plenty of paid and free parking options. To prevent fines, familiarise yourself with parking restrictions.

Water Transportation and Cruises

Because of the Arabian Gulf's extensive coastline and lively marine culture, cruises and sea travel are attractive ways to discover this dynamic region. The Gulf of Mexico offers a range of options to fit your vacation needs, whether you're looking to take picturesque cruises, go island hopping, or move between coastal locations. A closer look into cruises and boat travel in the Arabian Gulf is provided below:

1. Dhow Cruises: Experience the Gulf's coastline beauty in a unique way aboard one of these traditional wooden dhows, which are decorated with billowing sails and elaborate decorations. Dhows frequently conduct dinner excursions, offering a secluded location to savour regional fare while admiring cityscapes or picturesque shorelines. Dhow cruises are frequently taken on Abu Dhabi's Corniche and Dubai Creek.

2. Ferries and Water Taxis: Connecting different waterfront regions in Gulf cities, ferries and water taxis are convenient and beautiful ways of transportation. Reaching islands like the Palm Jumeirah in Dubai or

Yas Island in Abu Dhabi is made very easy by these services. They provide a novel viewpoint on the well-known sights along the Gulf.

3. Island-hopping excursions: The Gulf is filled with beautiful islands, each of which provides a different kind of experience. To visit places like Sir Bani Yas Island, Bahrain's Amwaj places, or Qatar's Banana Island Resort, think about taking a ferry or renting a boat.

4. boat tours at Dubai Marina: Dubai Marina is well known for its lavish boat tours, which offer an elegant way to take in the city's breathtaking coastline. For a special outing, you might rent a private yacht or go on a group cruise.

5. Coastline Sightseeing Cruises: A lot of Gulf cities provide coastline sightseeing

excursions that give you a great view of famous monuments. On these cruises, historical and symbolic explanations of the landmarks you pass are frequently included.

6. Dinner Cruises: On a dinner cruise, savour an evening of culinary treats and entertainment. These cruises, which are frequently conducted on cutting-edge vessels, provide a luxurious dining experience and live entertainment for couples or families.

7. Adventure Cruises: If you're an active traveller, think about going on a cruise that includes things like fishing, snorkelling, or scuba diving. A few trips also provide passengers the chance to see some of the Gulf's varied marine life, like dolphins and turtles.

8. Luxury Cruises: Treat yourself to a luxury cruise for an opulent vacation that blends opulent lodging, fine food, and top-notch facilities. These cruises frequently stop at numerous Gulf locations.

9. Educational & Cultural Cruises: A number of cruises offer educational and cultural excursions that provide a window into the culture, history, and traditions of the Gulf. You may find out more about local arts and crafts, pearl diving, and the region's maritime heritage.

10. Cruising Season: Cruising in the Arabian Gulf is popular all year round, although the winter season (November to April) is especially pleasant due to the milder weather.

CHAPTER 3

Exploring the Neighborhoods

Downtown Dubai

The bustling centre of Dubai, the city that defies the bounds of possibility, is located in Downtown Dubai. This magnificent metropolitan area, which is hidden beneath the iconic Burj Khalifa, is a monument to human inventiveness and architectural skill. Downtown Dubai, with its flawless fusion of modernism and elegance, serves as a symbol of the area's unrelenting quest for perfection.

Iconic Landmarks: The Burj Khalifa, the world's tallest structure, lies at the centre of Downtown Dubai and pierces the sky at an astounding 828 metres. Every traveller should go there because of the stunning panoramas that can be seen from its observation decks of the city. The Dubai Mall, a nearby shopping and entertainment haven with opulent boutiques, top-notch restaurants, and enthralling attractions like the Dubai Aquarium and Underwater Zoo, beckons.

Fountains of Wonder: The Dubai Fountain is a choreographed aquatic show that mesmerises visitors every day. It is situated in front of the Burj Khalifa and the opulent Dubai Mall. The fountain's jets blast water up to 150 metres into the air as it moves to music and lights, producing a kaleidoscope of colour and action that mesmerises viewers.

Luxury Living: Downtown Dubai isn't simply a tourist destination; it's also a place to live lavishly. Luxury properties with unmatched city views, like The Address Downtown Dubai, offer opulent lodging. Imagine enjoying a peaceful evening on your private balcony while watching the Dubai Fountain play, or waking up to the sight of the Burj Khalifa.

Cultural Oasis: Souk Al Bahar is a cultural oasis that can be found among the glistening skyscrapers. With its boutiques, art galleries, and a variety of restaurants, this typical Arabian market has a wonderful ambience. It offers a peaceful respite from the bustle of the metropolis.

Diverse Dining: Downtown Dubai offers a wide variety of dining options for food lovers. The neighbourhood offers gastronomic experiences to suit every appetite, from Michelin-starred restaurants to food carts selling delicious shawarmas.

Accessibility: The area is remarkably accessible, and the Red Line of the Dubai Metro serves a number of stations nearby, making it simple to travel to other areas of the city. Taxis and ride-sharing services are also easily accessible.

Downtown Dubai is a hub for entertainment and cultural events in addition to being a destination for shopping and dining. The Dubai Opera presents a variety of concerts, ballets, operas, and theatre shows with its spectacular architecture and top-notch performances.

The Historical Al Fahidi District

The Al Fahidi Historical District is tucked away amid the glittering skyscrapers and technological luxury that characterise modern Dubai, serving as a living example of the city's rich legacy and ongoing ties to the past. This charming area, also known as Al Bastakiya, offers a mesmerising trip through time where traditional Arabian architecture and the echoes of Dubai's modest origins transport you to a different time.

A Snippet of History: You must first go back in time to fully understand Al Fahidi. This neighbourhood, which was formerly a lively trading post and fishing village, captures the spirit of old Dubai. You discover its illustrious past as you meander through its maze-like alleyways.

The architecture of Al Fahidi's wind towers is one of its most recognisable aspects. These elaborate constructions are works of architecture made to make use of the cooling effects of the desert breeze. They delicately soar over the neighbourhood's rooftops, paying homage to old-school engineering prowess.

Al Fahidi Fort: The Al Fahidi Fort, a historical treasure from the late 18th century, is located in the centre of the neighbourhood. As the Dubai Museum, it now allows tourists to journey through Dubai's history, from the time of pearl diving to the oil boom that changed the city.

Al Fahidi has also developed into a centre for culture and the arts. Its surroundings are dotted with galleries and museums that showcase both domestic and foreign talent. A distinctive contrast between originality and tradition is produced by this injection of art into the ancient neighbourhood.

Cultural Immersion: Explore the cultural exhibitions that give information about regional customs, traditional dress, and the daily lives of the people who once lived in these alleys to properly comprehend Emirati heritage.

Coffee Shops and Courtyards: Find solace from the hectic city in the calm courtyards and old-fashioned coffee shops, which will greet you with aromatic Arabic coffee and delicious dates. These welcoming environments promote interaction with residents and other tourists.

Heritage Preserved: Restored historic houses that have been turned into cultural hubs and workshops for traditional crafts provide visitors with a chance to interact with Emirati traditions and pick up some of their abilities.

The wonder of Architecture: Al Fahidi's constructions beckon exploration. Its quaint buildings, courtyards, and winding streets give the area a timeless quality that is both alluring and charming. There seems to be a hidden gem around every turn, just waiting to be found.

Boutiques and Souvenirs: The area's boutique stores entice with one-of-a-kind trinkets including handcrafted goods, fabrics, jewellery, and regional artwork. It's the perfect location to find souvenirs that perfectly capture Al Fahidi.

Cultural Festivals: Keep an eye out for any festivals or events that occasionally line the streets of Al Fahidi. With lively displays of Emirati history, traditional music, dance performances, and music, these events animate the neighbourhood.

Jumeirah: Beaches and Luxury

Jumeirah, whose name is connected with wealth and a stunning coastline, is a beachside neighbourhood in Dubai that personifies grandeur and seaside relaxation. Jumeirah, which is located along the Arabian Gulf, attracts tourists looking for leisure, luxury, and unique beach experiences. Explore the sandy beaches and opulent amenities that make Jumeirah a refuge of both unspoiled nature and luxurious life in this chapter.

1. Jumeirah Beaches: Explore the shoreline of Jumeirah and take in the gorgeous sands and clean waters. Jumeirah Beach, Kite Beach, and Sunset Beach are well known for their immaculate beauty and provide a peaceful haven from the bustle of the city.

2. Luxury Resorts: Spend your stay at one of Jumeirah's luxury resorts to experience first-rate hospitality. These storied buildings provide breathtaking seaside settings, opulent interiors, and first-rate services.

3. The Burj Al Arab: See the renowned Burj Al Arab, frequently referred to be the most opulent hotel in the world. You can still

appreciate its unusual sail-shaped appearance even if you aren't a visitor.

4. Fine Dining: Indulge in gourmet fare at one of Jumeirah's finest eateries, which features a combination of ethnic flavours and cutting-edge cuisine. Many of these places provide breathtaking ocean views.

5. The beaches of Jumeirah provide a variety of water sports and activities, so get out there and explore. Every water enthusiast may find something to enjoy, from paddleboarding and snorkelling to jet skiing and parasailing.

6. Luxurious Shopping: Look into affluent shopping areas like City Walk and The Beach at JBR, where you may splurge on designer clothing, jewellery, and boutique treasures.

7. Spa retreats: Indulge in health and spa treatments at Jumeirah's premier facilities. While receiving massages and other restorative treatments while overlooking the ocean, relaxation becomes a whole new meaning.

8. Visit the magnificent Jumeirah Mosque, one of the few in Dubai that welcomes non-Muslim guests. The architecture and culture of Islam are revealed through guided tours.

9. Outdoor Promenades: Take a stroll along the shore's beautifully planted promenades. These are ideal for leisurely walks or running and offer beautiful views of the Arabian Gulf.

10. Sunset Views: Every evening, Jumeirah's beaches are graced by

magnificent sunsets. It's a peaceful scene to record or just enjoy with loved ones.

11. Nightlife: Enjoy the lively nightlife scene in Jumeirah at seaside bars and cafes where you can sip on beverages, listen to live music and mingle with other tourists.

12. Family-Friendly Attractions: Jumeirah offers family-friendly activities including the aquatic theme park Wild Wadi Water Park, which features exhilarating slides and rides.

13. Explore the contemporary art scene in locations like the Dubai Opera and the art installations along the Dubai Canal, where creativity and luxury converge.

14. Boat Tours: Take a luxurious boat trip or charter a yacht for a distinctive view of Dubai's coastline. There are possibilities for fishing, dining, and other activities.

Check the neighbourhood calendar for events and festivals that frequently take place in Jumeirah and offer a mix of culture, entertainment, and luxury.

The Modernity of Dubai Marina

Dubai Marina, a brilliant example of modern urban design and architecture, embodies the modernism and ingenuity for which Dubai is known throughout the world. This gorgeous area, which is situated along the city's unspoiled coastline, is a monument to Dubai's vision and resolve to develop a top-tier location that skillfully combines opulent lifestyle, cutting-edge technology, and stunning aesthetics.

1. Architectural Wonders: The skyline of Dubai Marina is unmatched. It has an astounding array of skyscrapers, each competing for the title of most beautiful architecturally. The city's modernity is defined by prominent buildings like the renowned Princess Tower and the twisted Cayan Tower.

2. Waterfront Living: The man-made canal, which is a key element of Dubai Marina, is surrounded by a number of opulent residential and business complexes. The layout of the marina enables people to take advantage of a distinctive waterfront lifestyle replete with personal moorings and promenades lined with yachts.

3. Amusement and recreation: For individuals looking for recreation and amusement, this area is a playground. In

contrast to the Walk at JBR (Jumeirah Beach Residence), which is a bustling pedestrian-friendly boulevard packed with cafes, restaurants, and shops, Dubai Marina Mall offers a wide variety of shopping and dining experiences.

4. Top-Notch Dining: Dubai Marina is home to some of the best restaurants in the area. You'll find a variety of culinary delights, whether your taste buds are tingling for international cuisine, seafood by the waterfront, or panoramic views from rooftop lounges.

5. Waterfront Activities: The marina's tranquil waters provide a backdrop for a variety of leisure pursuits, such as boat cruises, paddleboarding, and jet skiing. For a calm evening on the water, you can also board a classic dhow cruise.

6. Luxurious Accommodations: Dubai Marina offers visitors the option to enjoy sumptuous living with views that span beyond the Arabian Gulf or the city's magnificent cityscape. The area is home to a number of upscale hotels and luxury apartments.

7. The Ain Dubai, popularly referred to as the Dubai Eye, will soon adorn the skyline. Being one of the biggest observation wheels in the world, it guarantees breathtaking views and an amazing experience.

8. Events and Festivals: Throughout the year, Dubai Marina holds a number of events and festivals, such as outdoor concerts, food festivals, and international boat shows, enhancing the area's energy.

9. The Beach at JBR: The Beach at JBR, which is next to Dubai Marina, is a well-liked

location for swimming, sunbathing, and beach activities. It provides a tranquil counterpoint to the urban setting.

10. Nightlife: As the sun sets, the nightlife scene in Dubai Marina comes to life. For those looking for evening entertainment, there are a variety of options available, from chic lounges to energetic nightclubs.

11. Iconic Skyscrapers: Take in the engineering prowess of the top architects and building companies in the globe. The skyline of Dubai Marina features structures that push the boundaries of architecture and technology, creating a canvas of innovation.

Old Meets New: Deira and Bur Dubai

The districts of Deira and Bur Dubai are located in the centre of Dubai, where the old and present coexist together. These two ancient neighbourhoods provide tangible reminders of how the city developed from a small fishing community to a modern metropolis. Discover how traditional souks and old-world architecture blend with contemporary construction and a thriving cultural scene.

Starting your journey by crossing Dubai Creek in an abra, a traditional wooden water taxi, is the first step. This brief trip provides beautiful views of Bur Dubai and Deira and establishes the tone for your visit.

Gold and Spice Souks: Explore the maze-like lanes of the Gold and Spice Souks in Deira. These crowded markets, which provide everything from glittering jewellery to fragrant spices, have served as trading hubs for generations.

Al Fahidi Historical Neighbourhood: Continue on to Bur Dubai to reach this neighbourhood. With its wind-tower architecture and elegantly renovated buildings, this district retains the city's legacy.

Visit the Dubai Museum, which is housed in the venerable Al Fahidi Fort. You'll find displays within that show Dubai's evolution, from its pearl-diving heritage to its contemporary goals.

Al Bastakiya Quarter: Take a stroll through this neighbourhood known for its winding streets and classic courtyard homes. Here, cultural hubs and art galleries give the old area fresh vitality.

Visit the Sheikh Mohammed Centre for Cultural Understanding to become more familiar with the community's culture. Participate in educational cultural tours and talks while eating authentic Emirati cuisine.

Textile Souk: In Bur Dubai, visit the Textile Souk to shop a vibrant selection of textiles and fabrics. This market gives visitors a look of the city's trading history.

Heritage and Diving Village: Explore this living museum that displays traditional UAE lives at the Heritage and Diving Village. You can see artisans at work and discover the area's lengthy maritime history.

Sheikh Saeed Al Maktoum House: Take a look around this ancient home to learn more about the life of Dubai's royal family. The displayed artefacts and architectural elements are amazing.

Dubai Souk Al Kabir: Discover Dubai Souk Al Kabir, often referred to as Meena Bazaar, a bustling marketplace with a wide selection of commodities, including spices, jewellery, and textiles.

Cultural Events: Pay attention to the festivals and events that are frequently held in both Deira and Bur Dubai. These festivals feature traditional dance, music, and artwork.

Visit Al Seef, a waterfront promenade in Bur Dubai, for a dash of contemporary amidst the traditional ambiance. Here, you'll discover a fusion of modern dining and retail alternatives with traditional architecture.

Beyond the City: Day Trips and Excursions

The Arabian Gulf region offers a multitude of natural beauties, historic monuments, and cultural experiences just a short ride away, despite the fact that the glittering cityscape of Dubai is definitely attractive. Explore the varied landscapes and undiscovered gems that lie beyond the city limits by going on exciting day trips and excursions. Here are some unique day trip ideas to think about:

1. Desert Safari: Take an exhilarating desert safari adventure in the captivating desert that envelops Dubai. Get in a 4x4 and go over sand dunes, take in stunning sunsets, and have authentic Bedouin feasts beneath a starry desert sky.

2. Hatta Mountain Safari: Head to Hatta, a hilly region inside the emirate of Dubai, to get away from the city's bustle. Explore the Hatta Heritage Village to learn about traditional mountain living, take a trip to the impressive Hatta Dam, and try off-roading in the challenging terrain.

3. Al Ain Oasis: Travel to Al Ain, dubbed the "Garden City" of the United Arab Emirates. Investigate the luxuriant Al Ain Oasis, a place of many date palms and historic

irrigation systems. For a taste of history and culture, don't miss the Al Jahili Fort and the Al Ain National Museum.

4. Sharjah Heritage Area: Enter the nearby emirate of Sharjah to learn more about its extensive cultural legacy. Explore the restored mansions, museums, and the Sharjah Art Museum in the Sharjah Heritage Area.

5. Musandam Peninsula, Oman: Visit the Musandam Peninsula in Oman for a day excursion. It is renowned for its breathtaking fjord-like vistas. Take a fjord cruise across the clear waters, go snorkelling, and look for wild dolphins.

6. The East Coast of Fujairah: Fujairah is located where the untamed Hajar Mountains and the blue waters of the Gulf of Oman converge. Visit the historic Fujairah Fort,

take gorgeous drives over mountain passes, and see pristine beaches.

7. Abu Dhabi: Although not strictly speaking a day excursion, Abu Dhabi is only 90 minutes by car from Dubai. Visit the impressive Sheikh Zayed Grand Mosque, wander along the Corniche, and discover the vibrant cultural environment in the capital of the UAE.

8. Spend the day at Dubai Parks and Resorts for entertainment that the whole family will enjoy. Theme parks including Motiongate Dubai, Legoland Dubai, and Bollywood Parks Dubai are all part of this entertainment complex.

9. Jebel Jais, Ras Al Khaimah: For those looking for action, a day excursion to Ras Al Khaimah's Jebel Jais is a need. The longest zipline in the world is located there,

providing an exhilarating adventure amidst stunning mountain views.

10. Dubai Aquarium and Underwater Zoo: At the Dubai Aquarium and Underwater Zoo, which is housed inside the Dubai Mall, learn about the wonders of marine life. You can go through a tunnel here while being surrounded by fish, including rays and sharks.

11. Al Marmoom Desert Conservation Reserve: Discover the peace of the Al Marmoom Desert Conservation Reserve, where you can see wildlife, try your hand at sandboarding, or just take in the calm desert scenery.

CHAPTER 4

Accommodation Options

Luxury Hotels and Resorts

With a wide selection of extravagant hotels and resorts that redefine the meaning of luxury and comfort, Dubai is recognised for its lavish hospitality business. Dubai's luxury hotels cater to sophisticated travellers looking for nothing less than the best, offering everything from iconic skyscrapers with panoramic views to seaside getaways giving the utmost in leisure. Here are a few of the city's most outstanding luxury hotels and resorts:

1. Burj Al Arab Jumeirah: The Burj Al Arab is a recognisable image of Dubai's opulence and is sometimes described as the world's only 7-star hotel. This magnificent sail-shaped structure is perched on its own island and offers sumptuous rooms, personal butlers, and unrivalled ocean views.

2. Atlantis, The Palm: Located on the Palm Jumeirah, Atlantis provides a distinctive fusion of luxury and exploration. Visitors can check out the Lost Chambers Aquarium, the

Aquaventure Waterpark, and a variety of fine dining establishments.

3. The Ritz-Carlton, Dubai: This opulent resort mixes sophisticated Arabian elegance with Mediterranean elements and is situated in the Marina. Private beach access, top-notch restaurants, and a luxurious spa experience are all available to guests.

4. One&Only The Palm: Situated on the western crescent of the Palm Jumeirah, this upscale beachside resort provides a tranquil haven with private pools, villas that are completely sequestered, and outstanding dining at ZEST and STAY by Yannick Alléno.

5. Burj Khalifa: Located on numerous levels of the renowned Burj Khalifa, the Armani Hotel Dubai. Visitors appreciate the modern

elegance, individualised care, and convenient proximity to The Dubai Mall.

6. Four Seasons Resort Dubai at Jumeirah Beach: This beachside retreat offers understated elegance on the Arabian Gulf coast and features opulent suites, top-notch dining at Sea Fu, and restorative spa services.

7. Bulgari Resort Dubai: Located on Jumeira Bay Island, this luxurious resort fuses Italian design with Arabian ambiance. It offers exclusive beach access, breath-taking panoramas, and top-notch cuisine at Il Ristorante - Niko Romito.

8. Waldorf Astoria Dubai Palm Jumeirah: This resort radiates classic luxury against the background of the Palm Jumeirah. Visitors can relax in their personal cabanas or indulge in fine dining at Mezzerie.

9. Jumeirah Al Qasr: This opulent mansion, which is a part of the Madinat Jumeirah resort complex, conjures the splendour of an Arabian royal house. There are many dining options, a traditional Souk Madinat, and a private beach.

10. The Palace Downtown Dubai: This palace-style hotel offers magnificent rooms, proximity to the Dubai Mall, and a choice of upscale dining establishments. It is situated close to the Burj Khalifa and Dubai Fountain.

11. On the secluded Jumeira Bay Island, The Bulgari Resort and Residences Dubai offers opulent villas with private pools, a luxurious spa, and fine dining at Il Café.

12. Jumeirah Beach Hotel: A premium resort that welcomes families and offers breathtaking ocean views, immaculate

beaches, and a variety of eating establishments, including the renowned Burj Al Arab Terrace.

Boutique Inns and Guesthouses

Dubai is well-known for its opulent luxury hotels and tall towers, but it also has quaint, private lodging options like boutique inns and guesthouses. For tourists seeking to get away from the city's bustle, these hidden jewels offer a warm and individualised experience. Here are a few unusual and welcoming boutique inns and guesthouses:

1. XVA Art Hotel: XVA Art Hotel mixes art and hospitality and is situated in the centre of the Al Fahidi Historical Neighbourhood (Al Bastakiya). The resort has an art gallery, a garden café, and individually decorated rooms.

2. The Farm Dubai: Find solace in this serene desert sanctuary, where rustic elegance combines with unspoiled beauty. It is tucked away in Al Barari and features organic eating, tranquil grounds, and inviting guest accommodations.

3. Villa Rotana: This upscale yet cosy boutique hotel is located in the centre of

Dubai. It's ideal for both pleasure and business travellers thanks to its strategic position and cutting-edge aesthetic.

4. Desert Palm PER AQUUM: A tranquil hideaway with beautiful villas, a spa, and the Epicure restaurant, Desert Palm is a hidden gem surrounded by lush green polo fields.

5. On the East Crescent of Palm Jumeirah, this boutique hotel offers a tranquil seaside setting, holistic wellness treatments, and stylish suites with breathtaking views. 5. The Retreat Palm Dubai MGallery by Sofitel.

6. Rove Downtown: With a prime position close to the Burj Khalifa and Dubai Mall, Rove Downtown offers a boutique-like ambience and modern decor at an affordable price.

7. La Ville Hotel & Suites CITY WALK Dubai, Autograph Collection: This boutique hotel offers modern elegance and convenient access to dining and shopping. It is situated in the fashionable CITY WALK neighbourhood.

8. Al Seef Heritage Hotel Dubai, Curio Collection by Hilton: At Al Seef, you can immerse yourself in Dubai's history while enjoying the lovely ambience of the Creek and classic Arabian architecture.

9. The Canvas Hotel Dubai - MGallery: Located in Al Rigga, this boutique hotel blends contemporary style with Arabian influences to create a distinctive and creative atmosphere.

10. Rove La Mer Beach: This hotel is situated in La Mer, a well-liked seaside resort, and it offers a boutique-like

experience with a lively and beachy ambience.

11. Park Hyatt Dubai: This sophisticated boutique hotel offers a calm retreat with tastefully furnished rooms and breathtaking views. It overlooks Dubai Creek.

12. Armani Hotel Dubai: The Armani Hotel Dubai, housed inside the Burj Khalifa, offers a high-end boutique experience with opulent suites and access to the city's dining and shopping.

Budget-Friendly Lodgings

Although Dubai is well-known for its luxury hotels and upscale resorts, it also provides a variety of affordable housing alternatives for visitors who want to see the city without breaking the bank. These lodgings offer relaxing stays, practical locations, and reasonable rates so you can use your money to enjoy Dubai's attractions and activities. Consider these possibilities for inexpensive lodging:

1. Hostels: There are an increasing number of hostels in Dubai that give travellers on a tight budget a cosy and social setting. Private rooms or dormitory-style rooms are frequently available at hostels for a fraction of the price of hotels.

2. Guesthouses: Also referred to as bed & breakfasts, guesthouses are a charming and affordable option. They offer a warm, welcoming environment, frequently with local hosts who can share local knowledge.

3. Cheap Hotels: Search for hotels in the city, especially in districts like Deira and Bur Dubai. These hotels are a great bargain for

your money because they provide tidy, cosy rooms with the essentials.

4. Serviced Apartments: If you're planning a longer stay, think about renting a serviced apartment. Due to the kitchens in these apartments, you may prepare your own meals at home and save money.

5. Airbnb offers a variety of lodging alternatives, including apartments and rooms in Dubai. Airbnb also offers vacation rentals. Renting a vacation home can be a cost-effective option, especially for parties or families that are travelling together.

6. Capsule Hotels: There are now capsule hotels in Dubai that offer a distinctive and affordable experience. These small sleeping pods are ideal for road trippers looking for ease and budget.

7. Economic hotel chains from around the world are present in Dubai and provide consistent quality and affordability. The rates at these hotels frequently include breakfast.

8. Last-Minute Booking Apps: Use them to book last-minute accommodations and to save money. These websites frequently give discounts to customers who make last-minute reservations.

9. Off-Peak Travel: Take into account going on a trip when it's not as busy because lodging costs are typically lower. In addition, rates for midweek stays may be less expensive than those for weekends.

10. Negotiation: Don't be shy about lowering hotel prices, especially for extended stays. Many places that are affordable welcome haggling.

11. Read reviews and check ratings on travel websites to make sure the low-cost housing you select satisfies your standards for cleanliness, security, and general comfort.

12. Transportation Accessibility: To make moving around the city more practical and affordable, select lodging close to transit hubs or metro stations.

Short-Term Rentals and Apartments

Finding the ideal lodging when travelling to the Arabian Gulf can significantly improve your travel experience. Apartments and short-term rentals, which are popular lodging options in this area, provide an appealing balance of comfort, convenience, and cultural immersion.

Travellers can find accommodations that meet their particular needs and tastes thanks to the abundance of options accessible. The Arabian Gulf offers everything from cosy studio flats to roomy vacation villas to intrepid singles, families, and groups.

Short-term rentals are appealing because of the location. You have a variety of options, whether you want the adrenaline of a bustling city centre, the serene allure of coastal houses, or the peace of private neighbourhoods.

Often, the defining characteristics of short-term rentals are their size and comfort. These motels are perfect for lengthy visits because they often offer more space than standard hotel rooms. A fully furnished kitchen, separate living and sleeping quarters, plus conveniences like washers and dryers provide a comfortable atmosphere.

The affordability of short-term rentals is one of its most alluring features, especially for extended stays or bigger groups. It's frequently more affordable than reserving multiple hotel rooms, and the savings can be used to explore the plethora of sights and experiences the Arabian Gulf has to offer.

Living in a flat is treasured for its privacy and freedom. You can come and go as you choose, prepare your own meals, and relax in a living area, which helps you feel more like a resident than a visitor.

Additionally, short-term rental properties usually provide extra amenities like swimming pools, fitness centres, and round-the-clock security. These features enhance your level of comfort and relaxation, enabling you to engage in leisure activities on-site.

It's simple to reserve your short-term rental in the Arabian Gulf thanks to a wide range of web resources and neighbourhood property management firms. These platforms offer thorough listings, enabling you to find the ideal lodging that matches your journey objectives.

But it's important to be aware of local laws, which can differ from city to city, regarding short-term rentals. To avoid any issues during your stay, be sure the lodging you choose complies with the law.

It's recommended to make your reservations well in advance, especially during the busiest tourist times, to make the most of your short-term rental experience.

Maintain open lines of communication with your host or property manager as well because they may offer helpful advice, local knowledge, and speedy fixes to any problems that could emerge.

CHAPTER 5

Dining and Cuisine

Dubai's Culinary Scene

Dubai's culinary sector is a lively tapestry made up of various nationalities, creative chefs, and a never-ending quest for perfection. With the fusion of classic flavours with modern ingenuity, it has developed into a destination for global cuisine that is a feast for the senses.

1. Multicultural Melting Pot: Due to Dubai's special status as a crossroads of the world, there is a rich mix of international cuisines. Dubai's dining scene is a celebration of diversity, showcasing everything from the intoxicating flavours of the Levant to the tantalising spices of India to the exquisite tastes of Europe.

2. Traditional Arabic Cuisine: Enjoy traditional Arabic cuisine to fully experience Emirati culture. Try luscious kebabs, flavorful biryanis, and delicate lamb mansaf. Al harees and machboos are two popular Emirati dishes that shouldn't be missed.

3. Street Food Delights: Food stalls and carts selling delectable street food can be found all over the busy streets of Dubai. For

a genuine taste of the Middle East, try shawarmas, falafels, and manakish, or savour some freshly grilled seafood by the sea.

4. Luxurious Fine Dining: Dubai is home to a number of Michelin-starred and celebrity chef-run eateries. The city provides a variety of exquisite dining experiences, from Nobu's Japanese-Peruvian fusion to Gordon Ramsay's famous Bread Street Kitchen.

5. Food Markets and Souks: Take a leisurely stroll around the vibrant food markets and classic souks, such the Spice Souk and the Gold Souk. These bustling markets serve as a window into Dubai's trading history in addition to being sensory treats.

6. Dining with a View: Enjoy a meal while admiring the city's famous monuments. For a memorable experience, have dinner while

admiring the Burj Khalifa, the Dubai Fountain, or the Palm Jumeirah.

7. Dining in the desert: For a genuinely distinctive experience, think of combining a desert safari with a delectable barbeque supper at night. It's a chance to enjoy Arabian cuisine in a captivating environment.

8. International Cuisine: Due to Dubai's multicultural population, the international culinary scene is thriving. You can savour genuine sushi, indulge in decadent pasta, or discover the exotic tastes of Southeast Asia.

9. Food Festivals: Throughout the year, Dubai holds a number of food festivals and events that highlight the skills of both domestic and foreign chefs. These celebrations of gastronomy make it the ideal opportunity to savour delectable foods.

10. Fusion and innovation: The chefs in Dubai are well known for their innovative culinary creations. Discover creative recipes that combine flavours and cooking methods from other cultures to create an interesting fusion cuisine that is exclusive to the city.

11. Sweet Temptations: To satisfy your sweet tooth after meals, try mouthwatering Arabic desserts like baklava, kunafa, and maqamat. You may also visit foreign dessert stores that include handmade confections and well-known pastries.

Must-Try Arabian Gulf Dishes

Exploring the Arabian Gulf involves more than simply taking in the views; it also involves travelling across the region's varied and rich culinary environment. The gastronomy of the Arabian Gulf is a reflection of centuries of history, shaped by trade, culture, and the opulent bounty of the sea and the desert. Here are a few meals you really must eat if you want to delight your palate and gain a delectable understanding of the culinary history of the Gulf.

1. Shawarma is a well-known favourite that consists of thinly sliced, slow-cooked meat (typically lamb or chicken) that has been marinated and cooked. It is then wrapped in flatbread. Tahini sauce, fresh veggies, and pickles are frequently served alongside it to create a delectable explosion of flavour.

2. Biryani: Made with soft meats (such as chicken, lamb, or fish) and occasionally vegetables, biryani is a fragrant and savoury

rice dish. The Gulf version frequently incorporates dried fruits and nuts, giving the food a sweet and nutty flavour.

3. Machboos: Popular in the Gulf, this spiced rice dish is akin to biryani. It combines rice, flavorful spices, and dried lemon with slow-cooked meat, such as chicken or lamb, to create a delicious fusion of savoury and tangy tastes.

Four. Harees Harees is a filling and healthy dish that is produced by slowly boiling wheat and meat (often chicken or lamb) until they resemble smooth porridge. During Ramadan and certain events, it is frequently enjoyed.

5. Al Harees Lahem: This hearty and comforting Gulf speciality is made of slow-cooked lamb and wheat. It is generally

cooked during festive occasions and is a labour of love.

6. Al Madrouba: Al Madrouba is a distinctive dish made with rice, chicken, and a blend of spices and yoghurt. The end result is a meal that is typically eaten during Ramadan and is creamy and savoury with a unique texture.

7. Samboosa: Samboosa are crispy pastries filled with different ingredients such as minced meat, veggies, or lentils. They are similar to samosas seen in other regions of the world. They are a well-liked snack or starter.

8. Grilled Seafood: The Arabian Gulf offers a wealth of fresh seafood due to its long coastline. Particularly delicious are grilled fish and prawns, which are frequently

marinated in a spice mixture and eaten with rice or flatbread.

9. Luqaimat: This delicacy is a must-try for everyone with a sweet tooth. These little, deep-fried dough balls are topped with sesame seeds and date syrup for a sweet and salty delicacy.

10. Umm Ali: Umm Ali is a delicious delicacy with bread pudding-like characteristics. Layers of puff pastry, almonds, raisins, and sweetened milk combine to make this delicacy, which is warm inviting and ideal for sharing.

11. Arabic Coffee and Dates: A trip to the Gulf isn't complete unless you indulge in some Arabic coffee (gahwa) and date snacks. The dates add a delicious balance of sweetness to the robust, fragrant, and frequently cardamom-flavored coffee.

Fine Dining Restaurants

The Arabian Gulf is known for its top-notch fine dining places, where culinary prowess combines with a rich atmosphere to produce unforgettable gourmet experiences. The fine dining scene in the Gulf region offers something to please every palate, whether you're looking for cosmopolitan cuisine or traditional Arabian flavours. Here's a sample of what to expect from the area's excellent dining establishments:

The Arabian Gulf's fine dining establishments make no compromises when it comes to establishing a classy and opulent ambience. You may anticipate opulent dining arrangements, soft furnishings, and elegantly planned rooms.

Fine Dining: The menus at fine dining places are expertly and artistically designed. You can savour a wide variety of cuisines, including French, Italian, Japanese, and more, as well as Arabic and Persian specialties.

Gourmet Ingredients: Gulf chefs take delight in acquiring the best and freshest ingredients, frequently fusing locally grown food with imported delicacies to generate imaginative and mouthwatering dishes.

Tasting meals: Many fine dining establishments include tasting menus that let you indulge in a carefully chosen assortment of foods. These menus frequently use ingredients that are in season and highlight the chef's inventiveness.

Wine Pairing: Fine dining venues have large wine lists that offer a wide variety of foreign and local wines. Sommeliers with expert knowledge are available to make pairing suggestions that can improve your dining experience.

Creative Presentation: The way food is presented is in and of itself a work of art. Each plate is expertly arranged by the chef to be visually attractive, frequently with elaborate garnishes and edible flowers.

Culinary Innovation: Gulf chefs are renowned for their innovative use of traditional flavours and cutting-edge cooking methods to produce one-of-a-kind and unforgettable dining experiences.

Private Dining: Many fine dining establishments include private dining areas, which makes them perfect locations for celebratory events, special occasions, and private meetings.

Seafood Extravaganza: Due to the region's seaside setting, seafood is a common item on menus at upscale restaurants. You may savour seafood and fish dishes made with recently caught seafood.

Dessert delights are a delectable treat that shouldn't be missed. The Gulf's top restaurants are masters in producing magnificent sweets that are both aesthetically pleasing and delectable.

Reservations: Due to their ubiquity, it is advised to make reservations in advance at fine dining venues, particularly at busy times or on special occasions.

Traditional Arabian foods are served in some fine dining establishments as part of cultural dining experiences, frequently in a setting reminiscent of a Bedouin tent or with live music.

Views & Locations: Many fine dining establishments are placed in prime locations to provide stunning views of the Arabian Gulf, city skylines, or historical sites, which improves the whole eating experience.

Dress Code: Although there might not always be a rigid one, fine dining restaurants usually urge formal or smart casual wear to go with the expensive ambience.

Street Food Delights

Indulging in the region's variety and delicious street cuisine is one of the most alluring and engaging gastronomic experiences you can have. The street food scene in this area is a treasure trove of flavours and traditions waiting to be discovered, from the heady spices of shawarma booths to the sweet fragrances of freshly baked pastries. Here are some delicious street foods you shouldn't miss while you're there:

1. Shawarma: You must try this famous dish. On a vertical rotisserie, thin slices of marinated meat, frequently chicken or lamb, are layered, slow-cooked to perfection, then shaved off and placed within warm flatbreads. It's a savoury explosion, topped

with fresh vegetables and a range of sauces.

2. Falafel: A vegetarian treat prepared from ground chickpeas or fava beans, these crispy, deep-fried balls or patties are delicious. Falafel sandwiches made with pita bread, tahini sauce, and fresh vegetables are tasty and filling.

3. Manakish: Manakish, a spherical flatbread akin to a pizza, is topped with a variety of savoury ingredients like cheese, ground meat, or za'atar, a herb and spice mixture. In wood-fired ovens, it is frequently prepared by request.

4. Samosas are savoury pastry stuffed with spicy potatoes, peas, and occasionally meat. Samosas are a well-liked street food because of their tasty filling and crispy, golden skin.

5. Kebabs: Grilled meat kebabs, including lamb, chicken, and beef, are a common type of street cuisine. They frequently come with a side of rice, bread, or salad and are skewered.

6. Al Harees: Typically made with wheat and chicken or lamb, this Ramadan speciality dish is slow-cooked. It's traditionally eaten during the holy month and cooked for hours until it becomes creamy.

7. Luqaimat is a well-liked delicacy for anyone with a sweet tooth. To create a delicious contrast of tastes and textures, date syrup or honey is drizzled over these bite-sized, deep-fried dumplings.

8. Al Khabeesa: Al Khabeesa is a classic dessert from the Gulf region that is prepared from dates, saffron, cardamom, and

rosewater. It is frequently served warm and topped with nuts.

9. Fresh Fruit Juices: Grab a glass of revitalising fresh fruit juice from a street vendor to quench your thirst. There are several alternatives available, ranging from common selections like orange and pomegranate to more unusual ones like sugarcane and tamarind.

10. Karak Chai: A popular street beverage known as karak chai is an aromatic and spicy tea. While you explore the city, sip on this sweet and creamy beverage, which is frequently made with condensed milk and a combination of spices.

11. Grilled Corn: A straightforward yet filling street food, grilled corn on the cob is frequently spiced with butter and other

seasonings to create a lovely blend of flavours.

12. Arabic Sweets: Try the baklava, ma'amoul (shortbread-like pastries filled with dates or almonds), and basbousa (a semolina cake soaked in syrup) among other Arabic sweets.

13. Almonds and Nuts: Pistachios, cashews, and almonds are just a few of the roasted and flavoured nuts that street vendors frequently sell.

Dietary Options for All

The broad and welcoming culinary scene in the Arabian Gulf, which accommodates a wide range of dietary choices and requirements, is one of the great things about dining there. The Arabian Gulf offers a variety of mouthwatering delicacies to suit any palate, regardless of whether you're a meat lover, a vegetarian, a vegan, or have certain dietary limitations. Here is a look at some of the culinary possibilities in this vibrant area:

Traditional Meat Delights: The Arabian Gulf is a meat lover's heaven. Enjoy grilled lamb or chicken, shawarma, and kebabs that are delicious. Don't pass up the chance to enjoy dishes like Mandi, a savoury rice and meat dish, or Al Harees, a slow-cooked beef and wheat porridge.

Fresh Seafood: The Arabian Gulf has an abundance of fresh seafood due to its coastal location. Eat grilled fish, prawns, and lobster, which are frequently seasoned with flavorful Middle Eastern spices.

Vegetarian delights: There are many options available to tempt vegetarians' taste buds. Try foods like tabbouleh, baba ghanoush, hummus, and falafel. Additionally, a variety of lentil-based meals and stuffed veggies are available.

Vegan travellers have a variety of delicious plant-based options to choose from. Many classic foods, such as the Fattoush salad, vegan flatbreads called Manakish, and a variety of mezze (small plates), are by nature vegan.

Gluten-Free Options: Those who are allergic to or sensitive to gluten should not be concerned. There are gluten-free variations of foods like the rice and meat dish Mansaf. Additionally, a lot of eateries have desserts and bread that are gluten-free.

Dairy-Free Alternatives: You can still enjoy Middle Eastern food if you have a lactose intolerance or eat a dairy-free diet. Choose delicacies like grilled veggies, rice pilaf, and filled grape leaves.

International cuisines: Gulf cities are cultural mashups, and this is reflected in the variety of restaurants. A variety of international cuisines, such as Italian, Japanese, Indian, and others, are available, frequently with vegetarian and vegan options.

Heart-healthy options: Travellers who are concerned about their weight can enjoy fresh salads, grilled lean meats, and a range of dishes made with ingredients like fresh vegetables and olive oil.

Many restaurants in the Arabian Gulf are considerate of dietary sensitivities and can fulfil special requirements. Menus. Please feel free to let the wait staff know about your dietary requirements.

Street Food Adventures: Pay attention to the thriving street food scene. It is simple to have quick and wholesome snacks on the road thanks to the merchants providing fresh fruit, nuts, and other foods.

Specialty Restaurants for Dietary Needs: Some Gulf towns feature eateries designed exclusively for dietary requirements, such as gluten-free and vegan options. These restaurants provide a wide variety of foods that can be customised to suit individual tastes.

Food Festivals: Attend local food fairs and markets to try a range of foods and discover various cuisines all in one location.

CHAPTER 6

Must-See Attractions

Burj Khalifa: The Tallest Building in the World

The Burj Khalifa, which rises majestically amid Dubai's glittering cityscape, is both a great architectural marvel and a well-known representation of human creativity. This amazing skyscraper redefines what is possible in the field of engineering and design, rising to a height of 828 metres (2,717 ft). Instead of just taking the lift to the top, a trip to the Burj Khalifa is an exciting journey through ingenuity and aspiration.

Architectural Wonder: The Burj Khalifa, which was created by famous architect Adrian Smith, is proof of contemporary design. Its sleek, slender design was influenced by both traditional Islamic architecture and the natural shapes of the desert. The building's unusual Y-shaped floor plan maximises natural light and offers breathtaking city vistas from all directions.

Unparalleled Height: The Burj Khalifa, the world's highest structure, provides an unrivalled view of Dubai and its environs.

Visitors can take in breathtaking views of the Arabian Gulf, the wide desert, and the city's dynamic metropolitan environment from its observation decks.

The Burj Khalifa's "At the Top" experience offers visitors a trip that includes a high-speed lift ride to the observation decks on the 124th and 148th floors. These observation decks provide you with a bird's-eye view of the city, allowing you to take in the intricate urban design of Dubai and the tranquillity of its surrounding natural settings.

Light and Sound Spectacle: As dusk falls, a captivating light and sound performance that illuminates the Burj Khalifa's façade comes to life. The LED Light Show, a magnificent display that turns the tower into a canvas for breathtaking visual beauty, is a must-see.

The Burj Khalifa is not only an architectural marvel; it is also a thriving centre for culture and leisure. The structure regularly accommodates events and exhibitions, giving it a dynamic quality in addition to its imposing presence.

Dubai Fountain: The Dubai Fountain, a choreographed water show, is located right next to the Burj Khalifa and adds to its beauty. The fountains are a visual spectacle and dance to music, especially in the evening.

Beyond its architectural and engineering accomplishments, the Burj Khalifa represents Dubai's dedication to advancement and innovation. It stands for the city's will to break down barriers and scale new heights in every sphere of existence.

Dubai Mall: Shopping and More

The Dubai Mall, located at the foot of the famous Burj Khalifa, is a unique haven for shopping and leisure. This retail mecca, which covers an incredible 5.4 million square feet, is more than just a mall; it's a world of limitless possibilities where food, shopping, entertainment, and culture come together to create an amazing experience.

Retail Paradise: With over 1,300 stores catering to every conceivable taste and inclination, Dubai Mall is a shopper's paradise. This mall offers everything, from high-end luxury brands to worldwide fashion houses and regional artists. Whether you're looking for the newest fashion trends or special mementoes, it's the ideal location to indulge in retail therapy.

Souk Al Bahar: Souk Al Bahar is a traditional Arabian market next to the Dubai Mall that provides a contrast to the sophistication of the mall. Explore the meandering lanes here for a glimpse of Dubai's past as you buy carpets, jewellery, handicrafts, and Arabic perfumes.

Culinary Delights: The Dubai Mall is a culinary paradise with a variety of dining establishments to please every appetite. You can sample flavours from all around the world at casual cafés, food courts, and fine dining establishments serving international cuisine. Don't forget to sample Emirati cuisine to get a taste of the regional flavours.

Beyond dining and shopping, the Dubai Mall is also a centre for entertainment. You can get up close and personal with aquatic life, such as sharks and rays, at the mall's Dubai Aquarium and Underwater Zoo. Modern virtual reality activities are offered at the VR Park Dubai, and you may skate on ice against a desert landscape at the Ice Rink.

Dubai Fountain: The Dubai Fountain is a captivating sight to behold and is located in the waterfront area immediately outside the mall. The nightly performances of this choreographed fountain show, which is synchronised to music and lit by lights, delight audiences and create a magical atmosphere.

Art & Culture: The Dubai Mall's cultural offerings, which include art galleries and exhibitions showcasing both national and international talent, will appeal to art enthusiasts. It's a location where you may admire how tradition and modernity have coexisted.

Families with children will find many kid-friendly attractions to occupy the young ones. Kids may have fun and learn at KidZania, and the Dubai Dinosaur exhibit has a real dinosaur skeleton that captures kids' imaginations.

Fashion Avenue: Fashion Avenue is a posh area of the Dubai Mall that is home to renowned brands and designers for people looking for high-end clothing. It is a sanctuary for lovers of fashion.

Souvenirs & Gifts: If you want to take something home as a reminder of your trip to Dubai, check out the many souvenir stores and boutiques that sell one-of-a-kind presents, regional handicrafts and keepsakes.

The Iconic Palm Jumeirah

The man-made wonder known as the Palm Jumeirah, which is tucked away in the Arabian Gulf's sparkling seas, pushes the limits of human ingenuity and engineering. This famous palm tree-shaped island, one of Dubai's most well-known and daring constructions, embodies the city's desire to turn the desert into a tropical haven.

A feat of engineering, the Palm Jumeirah is a marvel. It took an incredible amount of sand and rock to build utilising land reclamation methods. A crescent, 16 fronds, and a trunk make up this architectural masterpiece, which was painstakingly planned to make the most of the available waterfront space.

The island is home to some of the most magnificent houses in the world, including pricey villas, condominiums, and five-star resorts. Residents and visitors can enjoy an unrivalled waterfront lifestyle with breath-taking views of the Gulf and Dubai's skyline thanks to its upscale properties.

The Palm Jumeirah is not merely a real estate development; it is also a centre for entertainment and pleasure. The island is a popular destination for locals and visitors looking for relaxation and excitement thanks to its selection of top-notch restaurants, beach clubs, and exciting nightlife alternatives.

Atlantis, The Palm: The renowned Atlantis, The Palm is located at the tip of the crescent. The Lost Chambers Aquarium, Aquaventure, an exhilarating waterpark, and unmatched luxury accommodations are all features of this legendary resort.

The Boardwalk: The Palm Jumeirah Boardwalk offers a beautiful strolling trail along the outer crescent for anyone wishing to explore the fronds. It offers numerous photo opportunities, breathtaking views of the Arabian Gulf, and an opportunity to enjoy the cool sea wind.

Marine Life Encounters: The waters surrounding Palm Jumeirah are crystal clear and filled with marine life. It's an excellent location for swimming with dolphins, scuba diving, and snorkelling.

Views of the Palms: Seeing the Palm Jumeirah from above is a once-in-a-lifetime experience. An unparalleled perspective of this unusual palm-shaped island is offered via seaplane excursions and helicopter trips. Initiatives for Sustainability: The Palm Jumeirah is a prime example of Dubai's dedication to sustainability. To reduce its impact on the environment, the island uses eco-friendly elements like water- and energy-saving technologies and lighting.

Future extension: The Palm Jumeirah is slated for additional development and extension as Dubai continues to change, providing even more opulent residential options and leisure possibilities in the years to come.

Dubai's Thriving Arts and Culture Scene

Dubai has developed a strong arts and culture scene that vibrates with originality, variety, and a profound respect for the arts in addition to its sparkling skyscrapers and opulent lifestyle. Dubai has firmly established itself as a global centre for creativity and expression thanks to the nurturing of a burgeoning cultural landscape in this city, which is noted for its rapid expansion.

1. Art Galleries and Museums: Dubai is home to an abundance of museums and art galleries that represent a wide range of artistic disciplines and historical eras. For those who appreciate art, the Dubai Opera District, Alserkal Avenue, and the Dubai Design District (d3) are important destinations. World-class productions, from opera to ballet, are presented at the Dubai Opera, which attracts performers from around the world and enthrals spectators.

2. The Dubai Opera House: The Dubai Opera House is the cultural hub of the city and is a spectacular architectural wonder. Numerous events are held at this top-notch location, including theatre shows, contemporary performances, and classical

concerts. Its design, which is reminiscent of the traditional Arabian dhow, gives its cosmopolitan offers a dash of local flavour.

3. Art Dubai: Galleries, collectors, and artists from all over the world are drawn to the internationally famous Art Dubai art fair. It provides a platform for both well-established and up-and-coming artists by showcasing contemporary art, modern masterpieces, and experimental works.

4. Literature and Poetry: Dubai has enthusiastically embraced literature and poetry. An important literary celebration that features prominent writers, seminars, and discussions is the Emirates Airline Festival of Literature. The city's artistic scene has seen an increase in popularity of poetry slams and spoken-word occasions.

5. The Dubai International Film Festival (DIFF) is a renowned film festival that features a broad selection of foreign and Arab films. Filmmakers, performers, and other industry professionals can use it as a platform to display their skills and engage with viewers around the world.

6. Local Talent and Creativity: Dubai's art industry cultivates local talent in addition to incorporating inspirations from abroad. Emirati musicians, entertainers, and artists are making their imprint on the world stage by incorporating their culture and experiences into their works of art.

7. Cultural Diversity: Dubai's cosmopolitan atmosphere is a wellspring of inspiration for artists, resulting to a fusion of cultures and artistic forms. Visitors can browse galleries featuring both traditional Emirati artwork and

more modern works that have been influenced by the city's multiculturalism.

8. Street Art and Urban Culture: Vibrant street art and urban culture animate Dubai's streets. The city's creative scene is enriched by the presence of vibrant murals and installations in places like City Walk and Jumeirah Beach Residence.

9. Traditional Performances: Arabic music, dancing, and theatre are just a few examples of the traditional performances that Dubai uses to commemorate its culture. Attend a spellbinding Tanoura dance performance or take in a mesmerising Arabic music concert that transports you to the Middle East.

Desert Adventures and Sand Dunes

Desert expeditions are a crucial component of the Gulf experience because the Arabian Gulf region is known for its huge, mesmerising deserts that extend as far as the eye can see. The Arabian deserts have something to offer every traveller, whether they're looking for exhilarating dune bashing or a peaceful desert getaway. Here's a peek at the world of dunes and desert adventures:

Hold hold tight as you go on a heart-pounding dune-bashing journey in number one. An adrenaline rush unlike any other is provided when expert drivers take you on an exhilarating rollercoaster ride across the massive sand dunes.

1. Desert Safari: A desert safari provides a well-rounded experience by combining dune-bashing with chances to see the desert's stunning natural features, such as its rare flora and fauna. As part of the safari, you can also attempt camel riding or sandboarding.

2. Sunset Spectacles: At dusk, the desert comes to life. A photographer's paradise, the sand dunes' golden tones. Many desert excursions involve a halt to take in this breathtaking natural display.

3. Stargazing: The Arabian desert offers clear night skies ideal for stargazing away from city lights. Sit back and take in the night's innumerable stars, a sight rarely encountered in cities.

4. Desert Camps: Spend a night in a desert camp to experience genuine Bedouin hospitality. With cultural events, delectable food, and cosy accommodations, these camps offer a look into the nomadic way of life.

5. Hot Air Balloon Rides: Take a hot air balloon ride above the desert to get a bird's-eye perspective of the breathtaking vistas. This serene encounter offers a distinctive viewpoint on the desert's size.

6. Desert Photography: Photographers have countless chances while photographing desert landscapes. Document the dunes' shifting hues and textures as well as the interaction of light and shadow.

7. Desert Flora and Fauna: Although the desert may appear lifeless, it is filled with creatures that have adapted to the harsh

environment. Desert animals, such as oryx, gazelles, and many bird species, should be seen.

8. Quad Biking: Crossing the dunes on a quad bike is an exciting alternative for people looking for an energetic experience. There is nothing like the sensation of flying over the beach.

9. Yoga and Meditation: For some tourists, the serene desert environment is ideal for practising yoga and meditation. The calm surroundings and immensity of the desert provide the perfect setting for relaxation and contemplation.

10. Festivals in the desert: If you're fortunate enough to travel during the annual Al Dhafra Festival or other similar occasions, you can see traditional Bedouin competitions, camel racing, and cultural

activities that highlight the close ties between the desert and the native way of life.

CHAPTER 7

Insider Tips and Local Secrets

Navigating the Souks and Markets

The chance to immerse yourself in the vivid tapestry of souks and markets that dot the cities and towns of the region is one of the most alluring parts of touring the Arabian Gulf. These vibrant, historical markets offer a sensory feast of colours, scents, and noises that transport you to a bygone age while also giving you a glimpse into Gulf culture and trade in the present.

1. The Souk Experience: Visiting a souk or market is more than simply a shopping trip; it's an adventure all on its own. These winding alleys are bustling with bustle as merchants advertise their wares, artisans showcase their talents, and the intoxicating scent of incense and spices permeates the space.

2. The Perfume Souk: Begin your trip with the Perfume Souk, where the enticing aromas of Arabian perfumes, oils, and fragrances will surround you. Allow the shop

owners to lead you through the world of Arabian fragrances; each has a special tale to tell and a seductive attraction.

3. The Spice Souk: Enter this veritable treasure trove of flavorful spices, herbs, and condiments by way of the Spice Souk. Saffron, cardamom, and other exotic ingredients that make up the core of Arabian cooking can be found here.

4. The Gold Souk: The Gold Souk in Dubai is renowned around the world for its extravagant displays of gold and jewellery. The glistening showcases are a sight to behold, whether you're looking for something special for a special occasion or you just want to enjoy the artistry.

5. The Textile Souk: At the Textile Souk, you may explore a world of luxurious textiles, vibrant silks, and delicate embroidery. This

is a site to savour whether you're looking for traditional clothing, or sewing supplies, or are just fascinated by the beautiful designs.

6. Bargaining and haggling: In the markets of the Gulf, haggling is an art form. Having a friendly barter with sellers is a great way to not only obtain a good price but also learn more about the community.

7. Local Handicrafts: Look around the stores that sell locally made items including elaborate ceramics, delicate glassware, and intricately woven carpets. Each object narrates the history and workmanship of the area.

8. Sampling Local Delights: Don't pass up the chance to sample street cuisine and local delicacies. The markets offer a wide variety of foods, from sweet pastries to

savoury nibbles, just waiting to be discovered.

9. Traditional Crafts: View craftspeople at work creating customary goods such as delicate metalwork, pottery, and rugs. Even some marketplaces include workshops where you may practise these trades.

10. Cultural Insights: Interact with local craftspeople and vendors to learn about the cultural importance of their items. Learn about the historical significance of particular objects or the symbolism behind certain designs.

11. Shopping Advice: Be aware that markets and souks are frequently busiest in the nights. Don't forget to bring a small bag or backpack for your purchases, along with comfortable walking shoes and clothing.

Understanding Local Etiquette

Understanding and observing local customs when visiting the Arabian Gulf is not only polite, but also necessary to guarantee a satisfying and culturally stimulating trip. The area is home to a diverse range of traditions and practises that are firmly anchored in Islamic principles and Bedouin culture. Here is a thorough explanation of regional etiquette to assist you in navigating social situations with dignity and respect:

1. Dress Subtly: In the Arabian Gulf, modest attire is highly regarded. Despite the widespread acceptance of Western-style attire, it's crucial to dress modestly when entering public spaces. This entails

concealing the cleavage, knees, and shoulders for both men and women. Women ought to think about putting on a headscarf when going to religious sites.

2. Greetings: The culture of the Arabian Gulf is characterised by cordial greetings. When meeting someone, shake their hand and say "As-Salaam-Alaikum" (peace be upon you) before shaking hands. "Wa-Alaikum-Salaam" (and peace be upon you) is the reply.

3. Public Displays of Affection: Kissing and hugging in public are considered inappropriate displays of affection and should be avoided. It's best to exercise control because even touching hands may be inappropriate.

4. observe for Religion: Due to the intense religiosity of the Arabian Gulf, it is crucial to

observe Islamic customs. Public places, such as stores and restaurants, may briefly close during prayer hours. If you are not taking part in the prayers, keep your silence.

5. Use your right hand for greetings, eating, giving and receiving things, and all social interactions. The left hand is historically regarded as unclean.

6. Removing Shoes: It's traditional to take your shoes off while entering a home or a mosque. Look for a specific space to put them in or take your host's lead.

7. Hospitality: The hospitality of the Arabian Gulf is legendary. When invited to someone's home, it's customary to remove your shoes before entering and to provide a modest gift, like candy or dates. It's always wise to accept gracefully because declining food or drink can be seen as rude.

8. Tipping: Tipping is customary, and it's polite to leave a gratuity in restaurants of about 10%, especially if service charges aren't included in the total.

9. When photographing people, especially women, always get their consent. Also, stay away from snapping shots of sensitive locations like military installations.

10. Public Conduct: Disorderly behaviour and public intoxication are not permitted. Alcohol drinking is permitted in specific locations, usually inside hotels and other legally permitted businesses.

11. Consider Ramadan: If your visit falls during Ramadan, show consideration for individuals who are fasting. Many places forbid daytime eating, drinking, and smoking in public.

Language and Communication Tips

Travelling to the Arabian Gulf can be enlightening and unforgettable, but in order to really appreciate your trip, it's crucial to understand the linguistic and cultural differences. Here are some language and communication hints to improve your ability to interact with people in other countries:

1. Acquire a basic vocabulary in Arabic:

Even though English is widely spoken, knowing a few fundamental Arabic phrases will help you connect with locals. It is courteous to use common greetings and phrases like "hello" (Marhaba), "thank you" (Shukran), and "please" (Min Fadlik).

2. English is Widely Used:

In the Arabian Gulf, especially in cities and popular tourist locations, English is widely spoken. Arabic and English translations of the majority of signage, menus, and government documents are available.

3. Script in Arabic:

Learn the Arabic writing system so you can understand menus, street signs, and some important information. Recognising letters might be helpful even if you don't understand every phrase.

4. Honour cultural customs:

Arab culture places a great priority on respect and politeness. Avoid being hostile or violent and speak to people politely. Be patient and keep your cool, especially under difficult circumstances.

5. Don't Overdress:

It's best to wear modestly, covering your shoulders and knees, in more traditional locations. Women should always have a scarf or shawl on hand so they can cover themselves when necessary.

6. The Holy Day is Friday.

Like Sunday in Western civilizations, Friday is regarded as a holy day. Particularly early in the day, a lot of companies and government buildings might have shortened hours or be closed.

7. Punctuality Matters:

In the Arabian Gulf, punctuality is highly valued. Show consideration for other people's schedules by being on time for appointments and trips.

8. Hand Motions

Learn the common hand gestures used in Arab culture, as well as what they mean. In your culture, benign gestures could be considered offensive in the Gulf area.

9. Make gestures with your right hand:

Since the left hand is typically used for cleanliness, it is considered courteous to give and receive objects with the right hand.

10. Market Bargaining: In local markets (souks), haggling is a frequent practice. When negotiating, show decency and consideration. Prices are typically negotiated.

11. Tipping Etiquette: Tipping is appropriate in hotels, restaurants, and other situations. Check your bills for service charges; if they are not there, leave a 10-15% tip.

12. Non-verbal cues, like a grin or a nod, are widely understood and can help people communicate across language boundaries. When appropriate, maintain eye contact since it exudes assurance and sincerity.

13. Always ask for permission before taking pictures of people, especially in more intimate or formal settings, out of respect for their privacy.

14. Be Aware of Religious practices: Show respect for regional traditions at prayer times, particularly on Fridays. Avoid playing loud music and acting disruptively.

Hidden Gems and Off-the-Beaten-Path Experiences

Despite the fact that the Arabian Gulf is well known for its famous landmarks and thriving towns, there are a number of undiscovered treasures and off-the-beaten-path experiences that are just waiting to be discovered. These lesser-known sights and activities offer a distinctive viewpoint of the area and a closer connection to its people, culture, and natural beauty. Here are some off-the-beaten-path attractions and hidden jewels that daring tourists should take into account:

1. Al Qudra Lakes (Dubai): Al Qudra Lakes is a man-made oasis in the middle of the

desert, where you can escape the hustle and bustle of the metropolis. Picnics, bird watching, and even stargazing are all ideal here.

2. Hatta Pools and Dam (Dubai): Take a tour of the charming Hatta region and learn about its undiscovered gem, the Hatta Pools and Dam. You can kayak, go swimming in the chilly water, or just relax and take in the peaceful surroundings.

3. Sir Bani Yas Island (Abu Dhabi): Sir Bani Yas Island offers a safari experience unlike any other. There is a wildlife reserve there where you can see giraffes and cheetahs grazing freely.

4. Al Wakrah Souq (Qatar): Al Wakrah Souq offers a more laid-back and conventional market experience, compared to the well-known Souq Waqif in Doha. Discover

the twisting lanes stocked with regional textiles, spices, and crafts.

5. Al Ahsa Oasis (Saudi Arabia): The Al Ahsa Oasis is one of the world's largest natural oases and a UNESCO World Heritage Site. Discover the natural springs, mediaeval villages, and palm trees.

6. Visit Al Khoudh Dam in Oman, a tranquil reservoir encircled by date palm farms and the Hajar Mountains. It's the perfect location for a peaceful picnic or leisurely stroll.

7. Kayaking in Mangroves (Abu Dhabi): Paddle through Abu Dhabi's Eastern Mangroves' mangrove forests to identify different bird species and take in the peace and quiet of nature.

8. Traditional Village of Al Hamra (Oman): Al Hamra lets you take in the allure of a typical Omani village. Discover the history and

culture of the area by touring the mud-brick homes.

9. Visit the Al Ain Camel Market in the United Arab Emirates, a bustling and genuine market where you can see the trade of camels, goats, and other livestock and get a sense of daily life there.

10. Jebel Hafeet Hot Springs (Al Ain, UAE): Take a relaxing bath in the healing waters of the Jebel Hafeet Hot Springs, which are located at the base of the magnificent Jebel Hafeet mountain and offer amazing views.

11. Camping in the Empty Quarter (Rub al Khali) for a fully immersive desert experience. The Empty Quarter is the largest continuous sand desert in the world, and it is located in Saudi Arabia or Oman.

12. Discover the tranquil Al Murjan Island in Bahrain, renowned for its immaculate

beaches, blue waters, and chances for water sport.

CHAPTER 8

Outdoor Activities and Adventures

Desert Safaris and Dune Bashing

Desert safaris and dune-bashing are two of the most exhilarating and iconic experiences that come to mind when you think of the

Arabian Gulf. This exhilarating journey provides a view of the vast, captivating desert expanses that surround the architectural wonders of cities like Dubai and Abu Dhabi. Here are some reasons why dune-bashing and desert safaris are must-do activities in the Arabian Gulf:

1. The Magnificence of the Desert: As far as the eye can see, the Arabian Desert is a mesmerising expanse of golden sand dunes. You can experience the magnificence of nature in its untainted, unadulterated state by exploring this particular area.

2. Dune Bashing: Driving off-road vehicles, usually 4x4 SUVs, across the sloping dunes of the desert is a thrilling activity known as "dune bashing." You'll experience a rollercoaster-like ride through the peaks and

valleys of the dunes as skilled drivers negotiate the sandy terrain.

3. Adrenaline Rush: Dune bashing is not recommended for the weak of heart. You'll feel an exhilaration and adrenaline rush as your car sprints up and down the dunes. It resembles an exhilarating theme park attraction that is situated in the middle of a desert.

4. Stunning Sunsets: Many desert safaris are scheduled to end with dusk, providing an unforgettable spectacle as the sun sinks below the sand dunes and bathes the desert in a warm, golden light. It's a lovely moment for couples and a photographer's paradise.

5. Desert Activities: Safaris in the desert provide more than just dune-bashing. You may experience camel riding, quad biking,

falconry demonstrations, and sandboarding to learn about the Bedouin way of life.

6. Stargazing: Due to its isolation, the Arabian Desert is a great place to observe the night sky. On clear evenings, removed from the light pollution of the city, you can be awed at the enormous canopy of stars above.

7. Cultural Experiences: A few desert safaris feature stops at authentic Bedouin camps, where you may partake in a sumptuous Arabian meal, get your nails painted with henna, and see tanoura and belly dancing performances, among other customs.

8. The desert is home to rare plants and animals that have adapted to the harsh desert environment. During your safari, keep a look out for desert wildlife such

Arabian oryx, gazelles, and various bird species.

9. Escape from Urban Life: A desert safari provides a welcome diversion from the hectic urban life seen in the cities along the Arabian Gulf. It offers a peaceful setting where you may relax and get in touch with nature.

10. Lasting Memories: A desert safari and dune-bashing trip in the Arabian Gulf promises to leave you with unforgettable memories and tales you'll tell for years to come, whether you're an adventure seeker or just looking for a singular experience.

Water Sports and Diving

Adventure seekers are drawn to the Arabian Gulf's clear waters by the abundance of thrilling chances for diving and water sports. The Gulf provides a wide variety of aquatic sports that are suitable for people of all skill levels, whether you're looking for the exhilaration of speed on the surface or the tranquillity of the underwater world.

Jet skiing: As you zoom over the Gulf on a jet ski, you can feel the wind in your hair and the sea spray. Jet ski rentals and guided trips are available in many coastal areas, particularly in Dubai and Abu Dhabi, offering an exhilarating experience.

Wakeboarding and Water Skiing: On the calm Gulf seas, test your coordination and balance by wakeboarding or water skiing. For beginners who want to master these sports, qualified instructors are available.

Kitesurfing: The Arabian Gulf is a kitesurfer's heaven due to its steady winds. Along the coasts, you may discover kite surfing schools that provide instruction for beginners and great conditions for seasoned riders.

Windsurfing: The Gulf's winds make it a popular location for windsurfing. Windsurfers of all skill levels can rent equipment and ride the waves, while beginners can receive lessons.

Paddleboarding: This leisurely method of discovering the Gulf's coastline. You can hire paddleboards and explore the water at your own leisure while taking in the tranquil views of the sea life and city below.

Kayaking: Take a kayak and explore the tranquil waters of the Gulf. You can take advantage of guided ecotours to learn about the area's distinctive marine environment and coastal scenery.

Scuba Diving: A remarkable diversity of marine life, including vibrant coral reefs, tropical fish, and even shipwrecks, may be found in the Arabian Gulf's warm and clear waters. Popular diving locations include Dubai, Abu Dhabi, and Oman, where licenced dive shops provide a variety of classes and guided dives.

Snorkelling in the Gulf is a wonderful experience for individuals who prefer to stay near the surface. There are numerous snorkelling spots near beaches and resorts where you may see thriving underwater habitats.

Fishing aficionados can go on deep-sea fishing expeditions to try their luck at capturing a variety of species, such as barracuda, kingfish, and others.

Yachting & Cruises: For a luxurious way to tour the Gulf coast, charter a private yacht or board a picturesque cruise. Popular choices include fishing excursions, dinner cruises, and sunset cruises.

Dhow Cruises: Take a leisurely voyage on a wooden sailboat while seeing the city's skyline and shoreline to experience the allure of classic Arabian dhow cruises.

Skydiving and Extreme Sports

Even while the Arabian Gulf is well-known for its opulent buildings and cultural gems, it is also a haven for thrill-seekers looking for thrilling experiences in the world of extreme sports. There are plenty of possibilities to make your heart race, from the enormous desert dunes to the turquoise seas of the Gulf. Here is an exciting overview of some of the extreme sports excursions you may take in this vibrant area:

1. Skydiving: Few activities can compare to the rush of adrenaline and jaw-dropping sights of skydiving over the Arabian Gulf. Imagine jumping out of an aeroplane, taking off into the air, and then falling freely over Dubai or Abu Dhabi's famous scenery. You'll always remember how thrilling it was to observe the Burj Khalifa or the Palm Jumeirah from above.

2. Desert Dune Bashing: Securely fasten yourself into a 4x4 car and set off on a desert dune bashing adventure. Professional drivers will take you on an exhilarating ride over the sand dunes, giving you an adrenaline-pumping experience with the captivating desert sunset as a backdrop.

3. Sandboarding: The enormous sand dunes of the Arabian Gulf provide the ideal environment for sandboarding if you're a snowboarder at heart. Learn to carve and slide on the supple sands as you down steep dunes. It's an exhilarating substitute for conventional winter sports.

4. Kitesurfing and Windsurfing: The Arabian Gulf is a sanctuary for fans of kitesurfing and windsurfing because to its steady winds and warm waters. For bikers of all skill levels, locations like Dubai, Ras Al Khaimah, and Bahrain provide ideal conditions.

5. Jet Skiing: Rent a jet ski and take to the waves for a high-speed adventure in the clear waters of the Gulf. Jet skiing provides an adrenaline rush with a hint of aquatic

exploration, whether you're racing along the shoreline or exploring uninhabited islands.

6. Paragliding: Fly like a bird over the breathtaking Gulf scenery while paragliding. Enjoy the sense of weightlessness while taking in the expansive views of the sea, deserts, and cityscapes.

7. Mountain biking: For avid mountain bikers, the Hajar Mountains in the neighbouring Sultanate of Oman provide difficult terrain. As you go across this breathtaking mountain range, you will have to negotiate rocky routes, uneven terrain, and steep descents.

8. Indoor Skiing and Snowboarding: Visit Ski Dubai, an indoor ski resort inside the Mall of the Emirates in Dubai, for a distinctive experience. Even in the sweltering heat of

the desert, you may ski or snowboard down slopes made of actual snow.

9. Rock Climbing: The Musandam Peninsula in Oman and Hatta in the UAE are well known for their options for rock climbing. Climb limestone cliffs for breathtaking views of deep fjords or take on strenuous Hajar Mountain climbs.

10. Scuba Diving and Snorkelling: Use scuba diving or snorkelling to explore the Arabian Gulf's underwater environment. Explore colourful coral reefs, shipwrecks, and a wide variety of marine life, such as fish of all different colours and turtles.

Golfing in Dubai

Dubai, which is renowned for its grandeur and spectacular attractions, has elevated itself to the top of the golfing world. This city-state, which is tucked away in the Arabian Desert, has turned its parched terrain into lush, green fairways, creating a golfer's dream. Dubai offers a golfing experience unlike any other thanks to world-class courses created by golfing superstars and excellent amenities.

Championship Courses: Dubai is home to numerous championship golf courses, all of which are intended to test and excite players of all abilities. One of the most famous golf courses in the city is the Emirates Golf Club, which hosts the annual Omega Dubai Desert Classic. Greg Norman's Earth Course at Jumeirah Golf Estates is another treasure that has played host to the DP World Tour Championship, an important competition on the European Tour.

Golfing All Year Long: One benefit of playing golf in Dubai is the year-round pleasant weather. It is feasible to tee off on Dubai's golf courses at any time, a luxury not available in many other golf locations due to the city's abundant sunshine and mild winters.

Golf academies: Dubai has world-class golf academies where seasoned golfers may hone their abilities and beginners can learn from qualified instructors. Modern technology and training facilities are available at these institutions.

After a round of golf, golfers can unwind in opulent clubhouses that offer outstanding dining options and breathtaking views of the surrounding landscapes. These clubhouses frequently present an opportunity to relax in elegance.

Golfers can tee off after sunset thanks to Dubai's night golfing experiences, which are played under floodlights, breaking with conventional wisdom. The game gains a new depth as a result of this singular encounter.

Golf Tournaments: The Omega Dubai Desert Classic and the Dubai Ladies Classic are only two of the major golf tournaments that are held in Dubai. Top golfers from all over the world participate in these competitions, giving spectators the chance to see their favourite players up close.

Background scenery: The contrast of Dubai's renowned skyline and the vast desert is one of the sport's most alluring features. This unusual setting produces an eerie atmosphere and amazing photo opportunities.

The golf courses in Dubai are recognised for their first-rate amenities, which include caddie services, golf cart rentals, and individualised support for golfers. A seamless and enjoyable golfing experience is the aim.

Environmentally friendly programmes: Dubai's dedication to sustainability is seen in the city's environmentally friendly golf courses. To conserve water and have a minimal negative environmental impact, these courses use cutting-edge irrigation technology and environmentally friendly landscaping techniques.

Accessibility: The majority of Dubai's golf courses are close to the city's top hotels and attractions, making it simple to reach them. Visitors can easily incorporate golfing into their time in Dubai because of this ease.

Wildlife Encounters

Wildlife interactions provide a priceless opportunity to re-connect with nature in a world where urbanisation and technology frequently rule our lives. This fosters a profound sense of awe, respect, and responsibility for the diverse ecosystems that share our globe. These interactions go beyond simple observation; they are portals into the complex network of life that envelops us.

Exploring Biodiversity: Wildlife encounters can take you deep into habitats that are teeming with biodiversity. These encounters demonstrate the astounding variety of life on Earth, from lush rainforests overflowing with diverse organisms to barren deserts where hardy species have adapted to harsh conditions.

aquatic Marvels: Exploring the globe's oceans' depths exposes a world of fascinating aquatic life. You can encounter brilliant fish, beautiful sea turtles, and the elusive beauty of sea anemones while snorkelling beside vibrant coral reefs. Experiences like swimming with dolphins or seeing mighty whales breach the surface make a lasting impression.

Safari Adventures: The African savannas provide renowned wildlife safaris where you can see the "Big Five" in their natural habitat, including lions, elephants, buffalo, leopards, and rhinoceroses. These safaris offer an opportunity to see animal behaviour, from a predator's thrilling chase to a family herd's sensitive moments.

Bliss of Birdwatching: Birdwatching offers a way to engage animals in a subtle yet profoundly rewarding way. Each bird species has its own tale to tell about adaptation and survival, whether it is the colourful plumage of tropical birds in the Amazon rainforest or the calm majesty of eagles soaring over mountain ranges.

Awareness of conservation issues: Educational elements are frequently included in wildlife encounters. Naturalists and conservationists are passionate about educating the public about the value of humans in maintaining environments and preserving endangered species.

Numerous indigenous societies have strong spiritual ties to the natural world. A holistic view of wildlife encounters can be gained through interacting with these communities, which can offer profound insights into the interconnectedness between humans and nature.

Wildlife interactions serve as a source of inspiration for photographers and artists who want to depict the beauty and diversity of life on Earth. They convey these experiences to the world through their cameras and paintings, fostering a shared love of the natural world.

Nature has an unmatched capacity to restore and revitalise the human spirit. Meeting wildlife invites you to take a break from the strains of everyday life and reconnect with your inner calm by allowing you to breathe in the fresh air and hear the sounds of nature.

Ethical and Responsible Encounters: The welfare of animals and ecosystems is prioritised in ethical wildlife encounters and responsible tourism. It's critical to select adventures that put conservation, sustainability, and the well-being of the affected animals first.

CHAPTER 9

Cultural Immersion

Museums and Art Galleries

The Arabian Gulf is a treasure trove of culture and history in addition to being a place of technological marvels and opulent skyscrapers. The rich tradition and artistic prowess that characterise the Arabian Gulf are showcased in the region's museums and art galleries, providing an enthralling trip through time. Here are a few of the region's must-see museums and galleries:

1. Louvre France and the UAE worked together to create this architectural marvel in Abu Dhabi (Abu Dhabi, UAE). Under its recognisable dome, it houses an incredible collection of artworks, comprising items from numerous civilizations and eras, creating a singular blending of cultures.

2. Dubai Museum (Dubai, UAE): The Dubai Museum offers a fascinating look into the city's past and is housed in the venerable Al Fahidi Fort. Traditional Emirati life, pearl diving, and Dubai's transformation from a small fishing town to a major world city are among topics covered in the exhibits.

3. Qatar National Museum (Doha, Qatar): This museum covers Qatar's history, culture, and natural environment through immersive exhibitions and interactive displays. It is housed in a magnificent modern structure modelled after a desert rose.

4. Sharjah Art Museum (Sharjah, UAE): This museum features the skills of regional and worldwide artists and is a centre for traditional and contemporary art. Additionally, it conducts cultural activities and ad hoc exhibitions all year round.

5. Bahrain National Museum (Manama, Bahrain): With artefacts dating back thousands of years, from ancient Dilmun to modern times, this museum provides a thorough insight of Bahrain's history and culture.

6. The I.M. Pei-designed Museum of Islamic Art in Doha, Qatar, is home to a sizable collection of Islamic artwork and artefacts from all over the world. The magnificent architecture of the structure is in and of itself a work of art.

7. Etihad Museum (Dubai, UAE): This museum protects and honours the history and heritage of the UAE's union and is situated near the Union House, where the United Arab Emirates was established in 1971.

8. Al Ain National Museum (Al Ain, United Arab Emirates): This museum in the "Garden City" of Al Ain displays the history of the area, including archaeological discoveries and cultural artefacts, and provides insights into traditional Bedouin life.

9. Mathaf: Arab Museum of Modern Art (Doha, Qatar): Mathaf houses a varied collection of works by Arab artists, including sculptures, paintings, and installations. It is devoted to modern Arab art.

10. Manarat Al Saadiyat (Abu Dhabi, UAE): This cultural centre, which is situated on Saadiyat Island, organises exhibitions, workshops, and events to advance the arts and cultures of the Gulf.

Historical Landmarks and Heritage Sites

The guardians of a country's past are historical landmarks and heritage places, which preserve tales, customs, and cultural riches for future generations. These locations give insights into the lives of those who came before us and the occasions that created our world, acting as windows into the history and heritage of a region. Here, we dive into these priceless gems' significance and continuing attraction.

Maintaining Cultural Identity: Historical sites and landmarks represent the soul of a country, expressing its own identity and cultural kaleidoscope. They serve as a reminder of the inventiveness, skill, and ideologies of earlier cultures, helping us to understand the richness and diversity of human culture.

A Peek into History: Entering the sacred grounds of a historical location is like travelling back in time. These locations take us to bygone ages, whether we are touring the magnificent Egyptian pyramids, strolling through a mediaeval European village, or admiring the beautiful carvings on ancient Asian temples.

Architectural marvels: Many historical locations are works of architecture that display the inventive methods and artistic talent of their designers. All of these buildings, from the magnificence of the Taj Mahal to the delicate mosaics of Istanbul's Hagia Sophia, are examples of human ingenuity and workmanship.

Heritage sites frequently have profound religious and cultural importance. They are sites of worship, pilgrimage, and introspection where customs are upheld and links to the spiritual world are made. Just a few examples of such treasured locations include the Golden Temple in Amritsar, the Vatican in Rome, and the Western Wall in Jerusalem.

Educational and Inspirational: Heritage sites and historical landmarks act as educational resources by providing insightful information on a variety of historical, artistic, and cultural topics. They pique our interest and light the spark of knowledge, enticing us to discover more about the tales they tell.

Tourism and Local Economy: These locations frequently serve as major tourist attractions and economic drivers. They boost cultural interchange, produce jobs, and instill a sense of pride in local communities. These locations bring tourists from all around the world, who enrich their own lives while contributing to the preservation efforts.

Preservation difficulties: Despite the incalculable value of these landmarks, they are not impervious to the effects of time, the environment, and human activity. To ensure that these treasures are preserved for future generations, preservation activities are essential. The World Heritage programme of UNESCO is essential in identifying and protecting these locations.

Historical landmarks and heritage places are a legacy that we leave for future generations. They serve as a link between the past, present, and future, serving as a reminder of the value of preserving our common history and the continuing force of human creativity.

Traditional Performances and Music

The Arabian Gulf is an area with a wealth of cultural traditions, and its traditional dances and music provide a mesmerising window into the hearts of its inhabitants. Through their rich artistic and cultural expressions, past generations have preserved the spirit of the Gulf's many civilizations and histories. The rhythms and melodies that have characterised this region for ages can be fully experienced here.

Traditional Music: The music of the Gulf is a fusion of Middle Eastern influences, with distinct rhythms and instruments that produce a singular sound tapestry. Traditional Gulf music frequently employs instruments like the oud, a stringed instrument, and the darbuka, a hand drum. It's a riveting experience that will take you back in time to see these instruments performed live.

The custom of pearl diving used to be the lifeline of the coastal towns along the Arabian Gulf. To coordinate their breathing and underwater motions, pearl divers sung songs, frequently to the beat of drums. These songs serve as a monument to the region's maritime peoples' tenacity and solidarity.

Yowla Dance: The Bedouin tribes of the Arabian Peninsula are the source of this ancient dance. It entails coordinated motions set to poetry and drums. At weddings and celebrations, the Yowla dance, a colourful celebration of Gulf culture, is frequently presented.

The Ayala Dance, which is performed by a group of male dancers with swords while dancing in a circle. The synchronised moves and rhythmic sword clashes pay respect to the area's martial history and traditions.

Al-Ayyala is a collective dance done by men during significant cultural events and festivities.It includes drumming, poetry readings, and coordinated motions. The community spirit and unity in the Gulf are reflected in the dance.

Al-Razfa is a lively and energising dance that is frequently performed at weddings and other festive occasions. Dancers do enthusiastic motions that radiate energy and enthusiasm while wielding conventional weapons like daggers.

Hudhud Chants are a type of vocal narrative that are frequently accompanied by drumming and other instruments. The oral traditions of the area are preserved through the chants, which include historical incidents, epic tales, and folklore.

Pearl divers sang pearling songs while they endured long sea voyages, which is number eight. These songs serve as a moving reminder of the struggles of the communities that depend on the sea for their livelihood as pearl divers in the Gulf.

Folklore and storytelling: Folklore and storytelling are an important part of traditional Gulf culture. "Hakawatis," or local storytellers, relate legends about supernatural beings, heroes, and moral lessons that have been handed down through the ages.

While maintaining tradition is important, current Gulf artists and musicians are also fusing traditional aspects with modern genres to create a dynamic fusion of old and new that represents the region's changing cultural landscape.

Learning About Dubai's Rich History and Culture

While Dubai is praised for its extravagant skyscrapers and futuristic marvels, it also has a rich and fascinating history that plays a significant role in shaping who it is now. Peeling back the layers of time to discover a story that spans centuries and connects tradition and contemporary is akin to exploring the rich tapestry of Dubai's past.

Historical Background: Over a thousand years ago, a little fishing and trading community called Dubai existed there. You can better understand how Dubai's unique location on the Arabian Gulf influenced its growth as a commerce hub by learning about its history.

Before the discovery of oil, Dubai's economy was based primarily on pearl digging. Explore the world of sailors and pearl merchants, their struggles, and their quest for these priceless gems.

Al Bastakiya, also known as the Al Fahidi Historical District, is a place that transports visitors back in time. You are transported to Dubai's past by the rebuilt wind-tower homes and the small lanes, which show you what life was like in the early 20th century.

Learn about the traditions and practises of the Emirati people to better understand their culture. There is plenty to learn, from the significance of camel racing to the significance of traditional clothes like the kandura and abaya.

The tools, gear, and tales of the once-thriving pearl industry are on display at

Dubai's Pearl Museum, which provides a thorough look into the history of pearl diving. Dubai Museum: The Dubai Museum offers an enthralling journey through time and is located inside the venerable Al Fahidi Fort. It has displays on Bedouin culture, the pearl trade, and the city's development into a major world city.

Immerse yourself in the cultural celebrations of Emirati customs at these festivals. A flavour of the local culture is provided via festivals like the Dubai Shopping Festival and Dubai Food Festival through food, art, and entertainment.

Heritage villages: Al Shindagha and Hatta Heritage Village are two examples of heritage villages that provide a look into Dubai's past. These "living museums" display customary arts and crafts, historical buildings, and everyday life.

Enjoy the flavours of Emirati cuisine, which are a reflection of the region's history and of the flavours of Arabia, Persia, and India. Enjoy meals like machbous, maqamat, and specialties made with camel flesh.

Find out more about Arabic calligraphy and the traditional arts of the Emiratis. The art of calligraphy is very important to the culture of the area, and it may be seen in numerous public places.

CHAPTER 10

Shopping in Dubai

Luxury Shopping Malls

Luxury shopping malls are important to this story since the Arabian Gulf is known for its lavish lifestyle and excessive shopping. These shopping centres are more than just places to buy things; they are also works of art, centres of entertainment, and exhibition halls for international fashion and design. Here, we examine some of the Gulf region's most recognisable luxury shopping centres:

1. Dubai Mall (Dubai, United Arab Emirates):

Overview: The Dubai Mall is more than simply a place to shop; it's also a luxurious entertainment complex. With more than 1,300 retail establishments, it's the largest mall by total square footage and provides a really exceptional shopping experience.

Luxury labels: The mall's dedicated Fashion Avenue is home to the most prominent luxury labels, such as Versace, Chanel, Louis Vuitton, and Gucci.

Beyond shopping, tourists may take advantage of entertainment options like the Dubai Aquarium, an ice rink the size of an

Olympic stadium, and the magnificent Dubai Fountain.

2. Dubai Mall of the Emirates

Overview: More than 630 international brands, including luxury merchants, can be found in the Mall of the Emirates, which is renowned for fusing shopping with entertainment.

Ski Dubai: A resort with an indoor ski area that lets guests experience snow and winter activities in the middle of the desert, Ski Dubai is one of the city's most distinctive attractions.

3. The Galleria (Abu Dhabi, UAE)

Overview: The Galleria is Abu Dhabi's premier luxury dining and shopping destination, and it is situated on Al Maryah Island.

This mall has a beautiful Luxury Promenade with recognisable names like Chanel, Prada, and Cartier.

Dining on the Waterfront: Savour waterfront cuisine while admiring the breathtaking Abu Dhabi skyline.

4. The Villaggio Mall in Doha, Qatar

Overview: The Villaggio Mall in Doha is modelled like the buildings in Venice and includes a canal within and gondolas.

Boutiques of the highest calibre can be found there, including Hermes, Valentino, and Dolce & Gabbana.

The mall also has an ice rink, a movie theatre complex, and an indoor theme park.

5. Bahrain City Centre, located in Manama, Bahrain

Overview: With a concentration on luxury and high-end brands, Bahrain City Centre is one of the country's biggest retail centres.

Premium variety: The mall provides a premium variety of high-end shops and restaurants.

6. Yas Mall in Abu Dhabi, UAE

Yas Mall, which is situated on Yas Island, offers guests a one-stop shop for luxury shopping, entertainment, and leisure.

Luxury Collection: You'll discover a carefully curated selection of high-end manufacturers, including Armani, Burberry, and Jimmy Choo.

7. The 360 Mall in Kuwait City:

Overview: 360 Mall is renowned for its cutting-edge architecture and selection of upscale retailers.

Luxury Court: The Luxury Court is devoted to pricey manufacturers like Dior, Chanel, and Louis Vuitton.

8. The Avenues, in Kuwait City

Overview: The Avenues, one of Kuwait's biggest shopping centres, offers a range of food, entertainment, and luxury retail options.

The Prestige: The Prestige section is devoted to upscale fashion and luxury products.

Traditional Souks and Bazaars

The Arabian Gulf is home to sparkling skyscrapers and cutting-edge shopping centres, but its old souks and bazaars are where the region's rich cultural legacy is tenderly preserved. These crowded markets, where traders have traded products, spices, and jewels for ages, are a living reflection of the past. A opportunity to travel back in time and discover the essence of Gulf culture and commerce, visiting these real markets.

1. Souk Al-Mubarakiya in Kuwait City is the first example.

Overview: One of Kuwait's oldest and most recognisable markets is Souk Al-Mubarakiya. It is a treasury of antiquities, textiles, spices, and regional handicrafts, among other traditional things.

Experience: Wander through little passageways and look around stores that sell expensive jewellery, fragrances, and rugs. The food stands serving delectable Kuwaiti cuisine are not to be missed.

2. Muscat, Oman, at Mutrah Souq:

Overview: The Al Dhalam Souq, also known as Mutrah Souq, is the most well-known market in Oman. It is known for its old-world beauty and is situated in the centre of Muscat.

Purchase Omani cutlery, fabrics, frankincense and one-of-a-kind mementos. When the lights turn on in the evening, the market is very lovely.

3. Gold Souk (Dubai, UAE)

Overview: Dubai's Gold Souk, located in Deira, is a spectacular display of gold jewellery and precious metals.

With more than 300 merchants, Gold Galore is a gold lover's dream come true, offering a breathtaking selection of classic and modern styles.

4. Spice Souk (Dubai, UAE):

Overview: Dubai's Spice Souk is a fragrant maze of aromatic herbs, spices, and conventional cures located next to the Gold Souk.

Explore a wide variety of aromas and flavours, including those of saffron, cardamom, exotic teas, and dried fruits. A sample is always gladly provided by vendors.

5. Doha, Qatar's Souq Waqif:

A lively market in the centre of Doha, Souq Waqif is renowned for its traditional Qatari architecture.

Shopping: Peruse the shops that sell anything from spices and falcons to clothing and perfumes. Traditional Arabic food and shisha are also excellent here.

6. Blue Souq (Sharjah, UAE)

Overview: The Central Market in Sharjah, commonly called the Blue Souq, is a stunning structure with a recognisable blue tile front.

Goods: There are numerous shops within that sell carpets, clothing, jewellery, and antiques. It's a fantastic location to discover Gulf and Emirati workmanship.

7. Souk Al Arsah (Sharjah, UAE):

One of the country's oldest markets, Souk Al Arsah provides a window into the country's commercial history.

Crafts: While taking in the historic ambiance, shop for handmade goods, antiques, and regional spices.

Manama Souq in Bahrain is number eight.

Overview: Manama Souq is a maze-like market that blends old and new in the centre of Bahrain's capital.

Treasures: Look through stores that sell gadgets, fabrics, spices, and pearls. It's a terrific spot to bargain and discover unusual goods.

Souvenirs and Unique Finds

There are several opportunities to find magnificent trinkets and one-of-a-kind treasures that showcase the Arabian Gulf's rich culture, traditions, and workmanship when exploring the region. The marketplaces and boutiques of the Gulf have something for any discriminating consumer, whether they are looking for traditional keepsakes or modern pieces of art. Consider the following mementoes and unusual finds:

Spice and herb markets in the Gulf are a sensory joy. The region has a long history of commerce. If you want to give your dishes an Arabian flair, buy saffron, cardamom, and different spice blends.

Handwoven Carpets: In the Gulf, handwoven carpets and rugs are highly cherished mementos. These ornate and vibrant fabrics frequently include conventional patterns that honour the region's cultural past.

Oud & perfumes: The Arabian Gulf is well known for its expensive fragrances and perfumes. The highly sought resin oud, which is also available in fragrance form, is a main component of many Gulf perfumes.

Jewellery: The gold and silver jewellery produced in the Gulf is renowned. Arabic calligraphy and complex patterns are frequent elements of traditional designs. Find one-of-a-kind items that highlight the workmanship of the area.

Camels are revered in Gulf culture, and their leather is utilised to make a range of goods, including bags, wallets, shoes, and belts. These premium leather products make wonderfully sturdy and distinctive gifts.

Consider buying abayas or kanduras, which are traditional Gulf garments for both men and women. In addition to being cultural emblems, these clothes are also cool desert clothing.

Henna supplies are available to help you make your own elaborate designs or temporary tattoos. Henna art is a beloved tradition in the Gulf.

Arabic calligraphy is a lovely art style, and you can find works by talented calligraphers that include lines from the Quran, well-known quotes, or your own personal sentiments.

Dallah Coffee Pots: These elaborate, traditional coffee pots aren't just useful; they also look beautiful on display.

Support local artists by buying paintings or other artwork that depicts the Gulf's natural beauty and distinctive culture. In large cities, look for galleries.

Historically, pearl diving was very popular in the Gulf. Despite the rarity of natural pearls today, cultured pearl jewellery is still rather lovely.

Arabian tea sets: Households in the Gulf region frequently display elaborate tea sets with exquisite designs. To reproduce the customary tea-drinking experience, think about taking a tea set home.

Handmade Pottery: Look through pottery stores for one-of-a-kind ceramic and clay products that highlight conventional Gulf craftsmanship.

Spa and wellness products: Look for locally produced spa and wellness items including organic skincare products, natural soaps, and essential oils that are frequently blended with enticing Arabian scents.

Antiques and collectables: For collectors, antique stores in the Gulf may have one-of-a-kind items such as antiquated books, antique jewellery, or historical artefacts.

Local Artisan Crafts

Investigating the world of regional artisan crafts is one of the most authentic ways to become immersed in the culture of the Arabian Gulf. The area has a long history of workmanship, where craftspeople have developed their abilities over many generations to produce stunning and one-of-a-kind works of art. Here are some regional arts and crafts you might want to look into purchasing as gifts:

Pottery: The fine pottery produced by Gulf artists is well-known. Ceramics with elaborate designs are available, ranging from colourful plates and bowls to ornamental vases and tiles. The rich colours and patterns of the area are frequently reflected in each piece.

Textiles: In the Gulf, traditional weaving and embroidery are highly prized crafts. Look for handcrafted fabrics with elaborate designs and skill, such as carpets, rugs, and tapestries.

Metalworking: The Gulf region has a thriving metalworking culture. You can find beautiful handcrafted jewellery, elaborately crafted cutlery and exquisite copper objects that are frequently inlaid with calligraphy and artistic patterns.

Woodwork: Gulf culture heavily incorporates woodcraft, and you can find exquisitely carved wooden doors, screens, and furniture. These items are truly works of art because of the exquisite craftsmanship and detailing.

Camel Bone and Horn: Craftsmen use camel horn and bone to make elaborate decorations. These unusual materials are used to make jewellery, cutlery, and decorative boxes.

Glassblowing: In the Gulf, glassblowing is a common craft. You can discover delicate glassware, such as vibrant vases and ornate lamps, frequently decorated with historical patterns.

Arabic calligraphy is a distinct art form in and of itself. Beautiful calligraphy is produced by artisans on materials like paper, canvas, and even wood. Verse from the Quran or well-known quotations are frequently used in these pieces of art.

Al Sadu Weaving: This age-old Bedouin method of weaving results in elaborate geometric designs on materials such as rugs and pillows. Aside from being visually stunning, Al Sadu products also have cultural importance.

Pearl Jewellery: Due to the region's long tradition of pearl diving, you can discover wonderful pearl jewellery, frequently made using pearls that were found nearby.

Oud perfume bottles: Oud, a highly valued scent in the Gulf, is kept in elaborate bottles that are frequently decorated with beautiful patterns. These bottles make interesting and lovely keepsakes.

Craftsmen make elaborate spice chests or boxes, which are often used to store priceless spices. They are works of art that are both attractive and utilitarian.

Traditional Dolls and Toys: Artists create traditional dolls and toys, frequently clothed in traditional garb, that depict Gulf culture. These are fantastic presents for kids or collectors.

Aluminium Art: Some artisans use recycled aluminium to produce beautiful works of art. These artworks frequently feature abstract or realistic scenes from the area.

Palm Leaf Crafts: Local artisans use palm leaves to make beautiful things like hats, mats, and baskets. These are not only useful but also highlight the area's ties to nature.

CHAPTER 11

Practical Information

Emergency Contacts

It's crucial to be ready for emergencies when visiting the Arabian Gulf or any other foreign country. Having the appropriate emergency contacts close at hand can give you peace of mind and guarantee you can get help if necessary. The following emergency numbers are crucial for the Arabian Gulf region:

1. Emergency Services: Dial 999 for immediate assistance in life-threatening situations. In a large number of Gulf nations, including the UAE and Qatar, this number

serves as the global emergency hotline. It links you up with emergency services like the police and fire.

2. Embassy or Consulate: Be aware of the location and phone number of your nation's embassy or consulate in the Arabian Gulf. They can help with legal troubles, passport problems, and crises concerning their residents.

3. Local Police: In addition to the universal emergency number (999), it's useful to have the non-emergency contact details for the local police. This is frequently available on the government website of the nation you are visiting.

4. Medical Emergencies: Knowing the location and phone number of the closest hospital or medical institution is essential in the event of a medical emergency. Also,

think about getting travel insurance that covers unexpected medical expenses.

5. Travel Insurance Provider: Keep your travel insurance provider's contact details close at hand. Included are the policy number, emergency contact information, and any other pertinent information from the insurance provider.

6. Credit Cards misplaced or Stolen: If your credit cards are stolen or misplaced, call your bank or credit card company right away. Ensure you have a phone or written note with your bank's overseas customer service number.

7. Roadside Assistance: If you intend to drive or rent a car in a country in the Gulf, be aware of the local roadside assistance service's phone number. In the event of a

vehicle breakdown, they can offer assistance.

8. Consular Services: Learn about the consular services provided by the embassy or consulate of your nation, including their contact information and hours of operation.

9. Tour Operator or Hotel: Keep the phone number of your tour operator or hotel front desk close at hand if you're on a guided tour or staying at a hotel. They can help with a range of travel-related problems.

10. Local Emergency Numbers: For specialised services like ambulance, fire, or police, several Gulf nations may have their own emergency numbers or versions of 999. Before your journey, do some research on these numbers.

Banking and ATMs

It's critical to have a thorough awareness of the banking and ATM services offered in the Arabian Gulf as you prepare for your trip there. The Gulf nations are renowned for their cutting-edge banking systems and widespread use of ATMs, making it rather simple for visitors to manage their finances while they are there. What you need to know is as follows:

1. Local Currency: Different currencies are utilised in the Gulf nations. Saudi Arabia utilises the Saudi Riyal (SAR), whereas the United Arab Emirates (UAE) uses the UAE Dirham (AED). There are other nations in the area with their own currencies.

2. ATMs: Throughout the Gulf region, ATMs are extensively accessible in towns and

cities. Along with local banks, significant multinational banks including HSBC, Citibank, and Standard Chartered are present here. Look for ATMs in hotels, retail centres, airports, and close to well-known tourist attractions. Most ATMs provide instructions in many languages and accept credit and debit cards from throughout the world, including Visa and Mastercard.

3. Currency Exchange: Airports, banks, exchange offices, and even certain hotels offer easy access to currency exchange services. Although it is convenient to convert money at airports, banks or exchange bureaus in the city centre may offer better deals.

4. Credit and Debit Cards: In the Gulf nations, especially in urban areas, credit and debit cards are commonly accepted.

Your cards can be used for a variety of things, such as paying for food, lodging, and other purchases. Carrying some cash is still a good idea, especially for smaller purchases or in more rural regions.

5. Bank Hours: Banks in the Gulf region normally have morning and early afternoon business hours, and they are open from Sunday through Thursday. Evening hours may also be extended at some branches in commercial areas. On Fridays and Saturdays, banks are closed.

6. International Banking: To prevent any potential problems with card security or access, let your bank know ahead of time about your travel dates and destinations if you intend to use your credit or debit cards frequently.

7. Currency Restrictions: Be mindful of any import and export laws governing currencies in both your own country and the Gulf nation you intend to visit. In order to prevent legal problems, it's crucial to abide by these regulations, which can differ.

8. Online Banking and Mobile Apps: Many banks in the Gulf region have online banking services and mobile apps, which can be useful for transferring money, paying bills, and monitoring account balances while on the go.

9. Currency Conversion: You can be given the choice to withdraw money in either your home currency or the local currency when using an ATM in the Gulf. In general, it's best to use the local currency to avoid having your home bank apply unfavourable conversion rates.

Internet and Connectivity

In order to communicate, navigate, and share your experiences when travelling in the Arabian Gulf, you must stay connected. Fortunately, you can stay connected while travelling thanks to the Gulf region's dependable and broad internet and communication alternatives. What you need to know is as follows:

1. Mobile Networks and SIM Cards: The Gulf countries have strong mobile connectivity with well-established 3G and 4G networks. At the airport or at shops and kiosks run by mobile service providers in cities, you can buy local SIM cards. These pre-paid SIM cards provide local calling and data services.

2. Roaming: Check with your home carrier regarding international roaming options for the Gulf region if you prefer to utilise your own mobile phone and plan. It's important to be informed of the expenses because roaming fees might be rather significant.

3. Wi-Fi: In the Gulf region, the majority of hotels, eateries, cafes, malls, and public areas provide free Wi-Fi. "Free Wi-Fi" signage is frequently seen, and joining these networks is usually simple.

4. Internet Speed and Quality: The internet in major Gulf cities like Dubai and Abu Dhabi is quick and dependable, in line with Western norms. The internet speed could be slower in more isolated regions, though.

5. VPN Use: Due to government limitations, access to some internet content and applications may be limited in Gulf nations.

Consider using a Virtual Private Network (VPN) service to get around restrictions if you need access to prohibited websites or apps.

6. Cybersecurity: Be watchful about cybersecurity when utilising public Wi-Fi networks. Avoid using insecure networks to access private or delicate information, such as online banking. A VPN could be used for more security.

7. Cost of international calls from the Gulf: International calls can be pricey. For more affordable communication, check with your mobile operator about their international calling plans or use web-based calling and messaging services like Skype or WhatsApp.

Internet cafes are still present in some regions, despite being less common than in the past. If you don't have access to a smartphone or laptop, they might be useful.

9. Mobile Apps: Before your journey, download travel-related apps, maps, and translation software to make sure you have the materials you'll need offline, especially in case you run into trouble with the internet.

10. Local Social Media and Messaging: The Gulf nations have widespread use of and access to popular social media sites like Facebook, Instagram, and WhatsApp. Utilising these channels makes it simple to interact with locals and keep informed.

Transportation Tips and Apps

With a variety of transport choices and practical mobile apps, navigating the lively towns and landscapes of the Arabian Gulf is made simple. This advice and apps will improve your trip, whether you're travelling to the desert or the cutting-edge metropolises of Dubai and Abu Dhabi:

1. Take advantage of the effective public transit options offered in the major Gulf cities. Route planning is made simple by real-time information about buses, trams, metros, and water taxis provided by apps like "RTA Dubai" for Dubai and "Darbi" for Abu Dhabi.

2. Ride-Sharing Services: Cities in the Gulf have easy access to Uber and other ride-sharing services. Use the associated app to travel yourself easily and cheaply after downloading.

3. cab Apps: The Gulf region's small-town cab companies also provide useful apps. To

schedule and track rides, think about using the "Careem" or "Yas Taxi" applications.

4. Navigational Apps: To go about the Gulf region, use navigational apps like Google Maps or Apple Maps. For driving, walking, and public transportation routes, these applications offer directions.

5. Metro applications: For cities like Dubai and Doha that have metro systems, specific metro applications offer details on train schedules, station locations, and ticketing alternatives. When visiting Dubai's metro system, travellers will find the "Dubai Metro" app to be especially helpful.

6. Car Rental: If you intend to rent a car, make reservations well in advance with trustworthy rental companies. Driving can be a practical option to explore less populated places in Gulf countries due to

their well-maintained road systems. If necessary, make sure you have a valid international driver's licence.

7. Parking in cities can be difficult, therefore parking apps are helpful. To search for available parking spaces and make parking payments online, use parking applications like "Mawaqif" in Abu Dhabi or "RTA Dubai Parking" in Dubai.

8. Purchasing a public transit card, such as the "Nol Card" in Dubai or the "Hafilat Card" in Abu Dhabi, maybe a good idea. You may reload these cards as necessary, and they provide simple access to a variety of public transport options.

9. Ride-Hailing Boats: In some Gulf cities, like Dubai, you may reserve water taxis or abras (traditional boats) via ride-hailing apps

for a distinctive and picturesque means of transportation.

10. Ride-sharing applications: In the Gulf, ride-sharing applications like "Carpool Arabia" are becoming more and more popular. These apps let you split the cost of transportation with other passengers.

11. Apps for Desert Safaris: If you're planning outdoor adventures or desert safaris, apps like "Arabian Adventures" in Dubai provide information and booking possibilities for exhilarating desert adventures.

12. Language Support: If you don't speak Arabic, language can be a hurdle. To make it easier to communicate with drivers and locals, use phrasebooks or translation programs like Google Translate.

13. Payment Apps: As many services and establishments in the Gulf allow mobile payments, make sure you have payment apps like Apple Pay or Google Pay set up on your smartphone.

14. Tipping: In the Gulf, it is traditional to provide tips to service providers including taxi drivers. To show your appreciation for the driver's exceptional service, round up your fare or leave a modest tip.

CONCLUSION

We hope that as we come to the end of our journey through the "Dubai Travel Guide 2024," you will be motivated and excited to start your own Dubai vacation. Dubai is more than simply a metropolis; it's a symphony of contrasts, where tradition and innovation coexist peacefully and the past whispers its tales amid the futuristic cityscape.

You've found architectural wonders that reach the heavens in the centre of this vibrant city, cultural riches that echo with centuries of history, and a vibrant tapestry of experiences that range from the serene desert dunes to the busy waterfront areas. This book has been created to arm you with the information and insights necessary to make the most of your trip to Dubai, a city of boundless possibilities.

Whether you're admiring the sparkling spire of the Burj Khalifa, indulging in a hearty Emirati dinner, or going on an exhilarating desert safari, Dubai provides a variety of experiences that will live in your memory for a lifetime.

But Dubai is a city with a soul—a place where traditions are valued, hospitality is a way of life, and creativity knows no bounds—beyond the lavish malls and opulent hotels. It's a location where you may shop for designer goods from around the world as well as bargain for spices in the crowded souks. It's a location where you may unwind on lovely beaches or go skiing on desert hills covered in snow.

We urge you to appreciate the city's diversity and immerse yourself in its rich cultural tapestry as you move across the bustling metropolis of Dubai. Talk to the people there, try their food, and discover their customs. Allow Dubai's distinctive fusion of East and West, ancient and new, to serve as your guide to a better, deeper understanding of this fascinating location.

Dreams come true in Dubai, where every visitor becomes a part of the city's always-changing narrative. The best experiences are frequently the ones that are unexpected—the hidden gems you discover, the connections you establish with locals, and the memories that remain long after you've left Dubai. So, as you bid farewell to the pages of this guide and embark on your journey to discover the real Dubai, keep this in mind.

It's up to you to heed Dubai's appeal to explore its promises of luxury, adventure, and culture. With the "Dubai Travel Guide 2024" by your side, you'll be well-equipped to navigate this vibrant city, make priceless memories, and set out on an unforgettable voyage of exploration. The opportunities in Dubai are as endless as the city's horizons. Have a safe trip, and may your time in Dubai be full of wonder, excitement, and wonderful experiences.

Printed in Great Britain
by Amazon

38216079R00145